# DATE DUE

# The Negro in the South

*His Economic Progress in Relation to
His Moral and Religious Development*

Being the William Levi Bull
Lectures for the Year 1907

By
**BOOKER T. WASHINGTON**
*Of the Tuskeegee Normal and Industrial Institute*
and
**W. E. BURGHARDT DuBOIS**
*Of the Atlanta University*

A UNIVERSITY BOOKS TITLE
PUBLISHED BY CAROL PUBLISHING GROUP

# Introduction

The book now in the reader's hands is quite unique; it is the only work which consists of the writings of Washington and Du Bois, the two giants of post-Reconstruction Afro-American history. Since these were public addresses, with all the time limitations that circumstance imposes, one finds here an especially succinct presentation of the contrasting views and techniques of the two men.

Internal evidence demonstrates that these lectures were delivered in Atlanta—Booker T. Washington at one point (p. 65) says, "Right here in Atlanta"—the time of their delivery was subsequent to the pogrom that occurred in that city in September 1906—for Du Bois refers to this outbreak (p. 115). And, since the publication date of the book[1] was June 1907, the lectures were offered sometime between October 1906 and about February 1907.

The qualities and ideas in Booker T. Washington that made him the favored spokesman for the Black population so far as Wall Street, Washington, and "enlightened" white

1. It was also published, in 1907, in London, by Moring, Ltd.

opinion were concerned appear in the essays that follow. One finds in them an acceptance of many of the racist stereotypes—imitative, primitive, docile, and so on—ensconced in stories and "jokes" together with an embracing of the entire mythology and ideology of Horatio Alger and Theodore Roosevelt. The references to "preferred" hair-styling and to the open-mouthed, reclining African "native" whose exertions extend only so far as masticating; to the heroic but impractical Indian as contrasted with the acquiescent but practical Black; to the status of the African stemming from his failure to adopt with sufficient intensity the lessons offered him by the white; to the assurance that with hard work all may prosper; to the assumption that it is material possession which is the aim of life; to affirmations whose divergence from fact can only be called breathtaking—"the Negro in the South has not only found a practically free field in the commercial world, but in the world of skilled labor" (p. 28) —all these endeared Washington to those in power. So, too, did his marvelously diplomatic references to slavery and his avoidance of any references to the realities of peonage, convict labor, lynchings, and mass murder—as in the city where he was then speaking—and his compliments to the extraordinary prowess of the white American (p. 74).

Above all, in Washington's attractiveness to the ruling class, were his emphasis upon "law and order" as the fruit of Tuskegee and his insistence that the securing of property was the road not only to salvation for the Black but also to serenity for the white. The securing of property assured property's security; this was basic to Washington's appeal and moved not only people like Booker T. Washington but also people like Moorfield Storey, the first President of the NAACP.

The down-to-earth, plain practicality of Washington was reflected in his somewhat extraordinary Gospel—that is, the three signs of Christianity were held to be clothes, a house, and work, which to the vagrant founder of that religion would surely have appeared as a revelation! Rather strikingly, here, Washington was presenting bourgeois values as synonymous with God's; this fit the dominant mood, for Bishop William Lawrence had greeted the twentieth century by announcing that "Wealth is in league with Godliness"— and the Bishop was an Episcopalian, just as were the sponsors of the lectures Washington was delivering.

There are two soft references to reality;

they come somewhat abruptly at the conclusion of each lecture. Closing the first, Washington suggests to his own brothers and sisters that "it is possible for a race, as it is for an individual, to learn to live up in such a high atmosphere that there is no human law that can prevail against it" (p. 41) ; the problem here is that the higher the atmosphere the more difficult becomes breathing.

And, closing his second lecture, Washington asks white people "to put their hands upon their hearts and then ask God if they were placed in the Negro's state, how, under the circumstances, would they like to be treated by their fellows. Conscience will answer the question" (p. 75). The problem here was that the "Negro's state" had endured for centuries with no significant impact upon that conscience; that the "Negro's state" was a social one with social origins and therefore social remedies; and that, in any case, if the basic Trinity of Christianity was clothes, a house, and a job, perhaps the Golden Rule was irrelevant.

While Washington had but eight years remaining to his life when these lectures were delivered, Du Bois had not yet reached his fortieth year and had before him almost five more decades of extraordinary creativity. In the immediate period of these lectures, Du Bois was teaching economics and sociology at Atlanta University, was General Secretary of the recently established and radical Niagara Movement, and had gained world-wide acclaim with his *Souls of Black Folk* (1903), his incisive essays (appearing in such periodicals as *The Independent* and *Collier's*), and his leadership in organizing the annual Atlanta University Conferences, commencing in 1896.

In his first lecture, Du Bois excoriated the system of slavery in the United States—a system which, he declared, "forbade machinery, discouraged human contact, and shackled thought" (p. 81); further, in a passage remarkable for its forthrightness—even from Du Bois—he commented that "the fathers of the United States" were so preoccupied with questions of commerce and politics, "they forgot matters of work and justice and human rights" (p. 81).

His extensive remarks on Reconstruction reflect the work that he had already published on that vital era and that was to result, after almost thirty years, in his magnum opus.[2] Already he was affirming that the effort of the Bourbon, after military defeat, was to come as close as possible to re-establishing slavery and he was pointing out the need for the introduction of real political democracy in the South if this process was to be halted and effective social change accomplished. Decades ahead of his time, then, Du Bois wrote: "This truth the great Thaddeus Stevens saw, and with a statesmanship far greater than Lincoln's he forced Negro suffrage on the South." Du Bois insisted that these new voters, "in the fundamental postulates of American freedom and democracy . . . were sane and sound"; and that the contributions of Radical Reconstruction were positive and noteworthy— viewpoints that only now are gaining currency within the historical profession (pp. 89–90) .

The defeat of Reconstruction led to the destruction of political democracy and the institution, said Du Bois, of a form of serfdom; the latter, he went on, remained the system dominant in the South as he spoke—that sys-

2. In the *Atlantic Monthly* for March 1901, Du Bois had published a pioneering essay on "The Freedmen's Bureau"; in the *American Historical Review* for July 1910 appeared his seminal "Reconstruction and Its Benefits" and in 1935 his great work, *Black Reconstruction*.

tem, he said, "is not a system of free labor; it is simply a form of peonage" (pp. 93–94). This was accomplished, he declared, because politics was dominated by the rich; in a passage as remarkable for its clarity as for its courage, Du Bois remarked:

Things were done quickly and quietly; they were done not for the good of people who had no political voice, but for the good of those who wielded the political power, *i.e.,* the business men and land owners. The laws were made to favor the landlord and the merchant and to make it easy to exploit the tenant and laborer (p. 93).

In reaction against this effort to reduce an entire people to serfdom and political impotence, they resisted, said Du Bois, in every possible way; of special consequence, he felt, was the appearance of what he here called "Group Economy"—"a cooperative arrangement of industry and service in a group which tends to make the group a closed economic circle, largely independent of surrounding whites" (p. 99). This thought—a basic insight into some of the specific features of the history of the Afro-American people—never left Du Bois and reappeared in the days of the Great Depression with his proposals for a

Black economy to assure the survival of the people.

Du Bois emphasized that the special oppression of the Black masses "had the sanction of great names of wealth and social influence" and that it was connected with the desire "to keep down the Southern white worker as well as the Black" (pp. 109–10).

Disfranchisement and legalized jim crow—and acquiescence therein, with the Black as a contented serf (essentially the Tuskegee arrangement)—were allegedly the means toward solving what was called the "race problem." But did it result in solution? Du Bois asked, and here he was frontally challenging Booker T. Washington. No, he answered; conditions had deteriorated for the Black and worsened for most whites and the South was more backward and had less favorable prospects after twenty years of the implementation of that "solution" than before. This was the basic reply to the "practicality" of the Tuskegee program; it was not practical at all for it did not work!

For a modern industry one needed modern education; urbanization and industrialization were coming to the South. Would they bring a decent civilization or not? If decent, education had to be of a top quality and skills had to be available for all—not least Blacks who would be facing the imperatives of advanced societies. In any case those Blacks would resist—were resisting (as Atlanta showed) — subordination and black-white unity was appearing and would grow: "It is only a question of time when white working men and black working men will see their common cause against the aggressions of exploiting capitalists" (p. 116) ; no doubt a longer time than Du Bois (and not he alone) thought likely nearly sixty years ago, but this was the direction of his plans and hopes and unfortunate it is that they have yet to reach full fruition.

With this vision and this analysis, it was clear to Du Bois that political power for the Black southern masses and the best possible educational system for them were required for their own advance and for the well-being of the South and of the nation.

Du Bois' second lecture—a considerable portion of which is quoted from the Eighth Atlanta University Conference for the Study of the Negro Problems (1903) on *The Negro Church*—emphasizes the basic challenge to American and Christian postulates represented in the oppression of Black people. "The paradox . . . which is daily stamping

hypocrisy upon their religion and upon their
land" (p. 179) is the fact that that religion
and those who rule that land refuse to consider the Afro-American person as a *person*.
But the personality is a fact, will never be
yielded, and must be faced up to by those
who are white or this nation will not survive;
that is the terribly contemporary message that
Du Bois offers in this lecture of nearly sixty
years ago.

Noteworthy in this lecture is Du Bois'
bringing forward the reality of resistance to
slavery that had marked the history of Black
people in the New World.[3] In this context,
too, is to be observed his obvious pleasure in
the fact that the white mob met effective resistance from the black community in Atlanta; it may be added that Du Bois himself,
while being away from the city during the
worst of the rioting, hastened back and
mounted guard, shotgun in hand, at the porch
of his home.

In this lecture, Du Bois emphasizes a point
that grew in his mind as he aged—namely,
the world-wide nature of the question of rac-
ism. "It is not a problem simply of the South,"

3. In 1907 Du Bois undertook a biography of John Brown
and this was published in 1909 by George W. Jacobs—
the original publishers of the present volume.

he remarks here, "not a problem simply of this country, it is a problem of the world" (p. 190).

The forthrightness of Du Bois was extraordinary; he would say exactly what was on his mind and say it with unsurpassed clarity at every opportunity and under all circumstances. Here he is, then, a Black man in Georgia in the first decade of the twentieth century—shortly after lynch mobs have ravaged the very city in which he is speaking—and he says:

It is absurd to call the practical religion of this nation Christian. We are not humble, we are impudently proud; we are not merciful, we are unmerciful toward friend and foe; we are not peaceful nor peacefully inclined as our armies and battle-ships declare; we do not want to be martyrs, we would much rather be thieves and liars so long as we can be rich; we do not seek continuously, and prayerfully inculcate, love and justice for our fellow men, but on the contrary the treatment of the poor, the unfortunate, and the black within our borders is almost a national crime (p. 186).

This book is remarkably free of typographical or technical slips. An occasional mistake appears, as on page 72, in the first full paragraph, the opening word obviously should be *May*, not *My;* Du Bois' note 24, on page 218, should be to *De Bow's Review,* Vol. XII, not II; strangely, too, the name *Tuskegee* is misspelled throughout, including on the title page.

Some of the quoted material in Du Bois' second essay (pp. 145–47) comes from the contribution by John Wesley Cromwell,[4] first published by Du Bois in No. 8 of the already mentioned Atlanta University Studies (1903).

The "Southern writer" quoted by Du Bois (pp. 149–52) is James Curtis Ballagh, from his *A History of Slavery in Virginia,* issued in 1902 by The Johns Hopkins University Press.

Both Washington and Du Bois mention the names—and often only the surnames—of several people; some note about these may be of use, ignoring relatively well-known figures like John Randolph of Virginia and Thaddeus Stevens of Pennsylvania:

ALDERMAN, EDWIN ANDERSON (1861–1931), mentioned on page 219, was a leading Southern educator, President of the University of

4. John W. Cromwell was born in slavery in Virginia in 1846. He became a well-known teacher and government employee in Washington, D.C., and published extensively; perhaps his best-known work was *The Negro in American History* (Washington, D.C.: American Negro Academy, 1914).

North Carolina (1896–1900); of Tulane (1900–1904); and of the University of Virginia (1904–31).

ARMSTRONG, SAMUEL CHAPMAN (1839–93), mentioned on page 46, was a Major-General in the United States Army during the Civil War, the Virginia agent of the Freedmen's Bureau after the war, and persuaded the American Missionary Association to found— with himself in charge—Hampton Institute in 1868, which he headed until his death.

BASSETT, JOHN SPENCER (1867–1928), of North Carolina, taught at Trinity (later called Duke) from 1894–1906; author of *Slavery and Servitude in North Carolina* (1896) and of *Anti-Slavery Leaders in North Carolina* (1898) and other books. Founding editor (1902) of the *South Atlantic Quarterly;* his editorial in a 1903 number (II,4) of that journal, "Stirring Up the Fires of Race Antipathy," in which Afro-American contemporary struggles were compared with struggles of oppressed people throughout history, led to a demand for his removal from his college post. This was resisted, but in 1906 he went to Smith College. He is referred to on page 219.

CRANDALL, PRUDENCE school is referred to on page 203. Miss Crandall, a Quaker, opened a school for girls in 1831 in Canterbury, Connecticut; in 1833 she admitted a Negro girl who lived in that state. Some parents objected and a campaign of harassment followed which culminated in the law to which Du Bois refers (p. 202). Miss Crandall was convicted of violating this law but the state's highest court voided the conviction; thereafter a mob destroyed the school.

DIXON, THOMAS (1864–1946), mentioned on pages 111 and 219, was the author of very influential and blatantly racist novels, particularly *The Leopard's Spots,* first published by Grosset & Dunlap in 1902; and *The Clansman; An Historical Romance of the Ku Klux Klan,* first published by Doubleday, Page, in 1905. The latter novel was the basis for the motion picture *Birth of a Nation,* released in 1915 and glorifying the KKK.

FLEMING, WALTER LYNWOOD (1874–1932) of Alabama, mentioned on page 218, was a well-known historian; just prior to the appearance of the present book, his two-volume study, *Documentary History of Reconstruction,* was published by A. H. Clark in Cleveland (1906–1907).

FRISSELL, HOLLIS BURKE (1851–1917), mentioned on page 65, began his career as Assist-
ant Pastor at the Madison Avenue Presbyterian Church in New York; he became Chap-
lain at Hampton Institute (1880–1893) and
succeeded General Armstrong as its Principal
(1893–1917). Dr. Frissell originated the conferences on education first held at Capon
Springs, West Virginia, in 1898, out of which
came the influential Southern Education
Board in 1901.

HARRIS, JOEL CHANDLER (1848–1908), men-
tioned on page 64, was connected with the
*Atlanta Constitution* from 1876 through 1900
and was the author of the best-selling *Uncle
Remus: His Songs and Sayings* (1881) and
*Nights With Uncle Remus* (1883).

MILLER, THOMAS EZEKIEL (1849–1938), mentioned on page 207, was born free in South
Carolina, graduated Lincoln University (Pa.),
became an attorney, and practiced in Beau-
fort, S. C. He was a member of the State
House and Senate in South Carolina in the
1870s and 1880s and a Member of the House
of Representatives, 1888–90. From 1896 to
1911 he was President of the State College
for Negroes at Orangeburg, S. C.

MURPHY, EDGAR GARDNER (1869–1913), mentioned on page 218, born in Arkansas, was an Episcopal clergyman who served as rector in Texas, Ohio, New York, and Alabama. He was organizer and secretary of an early interracial Southern conference, held in 1900 in Montgomery, Alabama, and was Executive Secretary of the Southern Education Board (1903–1908); in 1904 he published a book with wide influence in its day, *Problems of the Present South.*

PAGE, THOMAS NELSON (1853–1922), referred to as Nelson Page on page 111, was a Virginia attorney and author, several of his stories and novels being written in so-called "Negro dialect." Among his best-selling novels was *In Ole Virginia* (1887); two of his nonfiction books were *The Old South* (1892) and *The Negro, The Southerner's Problem* (1904). Page was Wilson's Ambassador to Italy from 1913 to 1919.

TILLMAN, BENJAMIN RYAN (1847–1918), mentioned on pages 111 and 219, was a South Carolina planter. He was Governor 1890–94, and U. S. Senator from 1895 until his death; he was a notorious racist.

TOURGEE, ALBION WINEGAR (1838–1905), mentioned on page 206, a lawyer and soldier (twice wounded in the Civil War), was a leader of Radical Reconstruction efforts in North Carolina, serving as a judge there from 1868 to 1874. He moved north in 1879 and wrote several novels of which two in particular had wide impact: *A Fool's Errand* (1879; reprinted by Harvard University Press in 1961, with an introduction by John Hope Franklin); and *Bricks Without Straw* (1880; reprinted in 1969 by Louisiana State University Press, with an introduction by his biographer, Otto H. Olsen).

VARDAMAN, JAMES KIMBLE (1861–1930), mentioned on pages 111 and 219, was a Mississippi lawyer and newspaperman. He was Governor (1904–1907) and U. S. Senator (1913–19). He was as vicious a racist as U. S. history knows.

WILLIAMS, JOHN SHARP (1854–1932), mentioned on page 209, was a Mississippi planter and politician, who entered Congress in 1893, served as Minority Leader, and was a Senator from 1911 to 1921. While not as crude as Tillman or Vardaman, he was openly racist.

There are several references to sources in Du Bois' essays and notes that require fuller presentation.

On pages 205–206 material is quoted from an article by Gilbert T. Stephenson, "Racial Distinctions in Southern Law," *American Political Science Review* I, (November 1906), 44–61.

On page 198 the reference to the work by Baines is to Edward Baines' *History of the Cotton Manufacture in Great Britain* (London, 1835, reprinted in New York in 1966 by A. M. Kelley).

The reference to the work by Blaine (p. 205) is to that by the well-known nineteenth-century Republican politician, James Gillespie Blaine, *Twenty Years of Congress: From Lincoln to Garfield,* 2 vols. (Norwich, Conn.: 1888).

The quoted material on pages 156–60 is from the work by the distinguished Negro attorney and author Archibald Henry Grimké (1849–1930) (President of the American Negro Academy, 1903–16), *Right on the Scaffold; or, The Martyrs of 1822.* This was an account of the Vesey slave conspiracy in South Carolina, published by the Academy in Washington in 1901.

The reference on page 218 to Fitzhugh is to George Fitzhugh (1806–81) a Virginia slaveowner, lawyer, and sociologist; the book cited is *Cannibals All!; Or Slaves Without*

*Masters,* first published in 1857 (reprinted in 1960 by Harvard University Press with a preface by C. Vann Woodward, and the same year in paper by Putnam's, with a preface by the late Harvey Wish).

Quoted material on pages 206–208 comes from John L. Love, *The Disfranchisement of the Negro,* Occasional Paper #6 of the American Negro Academy (Washington, 1899).

On pages 214–17, material is cited as taken from the history of the Society for the Propagation of the Gospel; this has reference to C. F. Pascow, *Two Hundred Years of the S.P.G.: An Historical Account of the Society for the Propagation of the Gospel in Foreign Parts, 1701–1900,* published by the Society in London in 1901 in two volumes.

The citation on page 218 to a book by Weeks is to Stephen B. Weeks, *Southern Quakers and Slavery* (Baltimore: Johns Hopkins University Press, 1896).

The material on pages 160–65, dealing with Nat Turner's slave rebellion (in Virginia in 1831) is cited as from the Atlanta University Publications, No. 8; in that source, in turn, what is used is the work of George W. Williams, *History of the Negro Race in America from 1619 to 1880,* 2 vols. (New York: Put-

nam's, 1882) , II, 85ff., and it is Mr. Williams
who is quoted by Du Bois.

Finally, readers may well wish additional
information concerning Du Bois' references
to black-white unity among Alabama miners
(pp. 116 and 212) . They should consult W.
E. B. Du Bois and Augustus G. Dill, eds.,
*The Negro American Artisan,* Atlanta University Publications No. 17 (Atlanta, 1912) ;
and Paul B. Worthman, "Black Workers and
Labor Unions in Birmingham, Alabama,
1897–1904," in *Labor History,* X (Summer
1969) , 375–407.

HERBERT APTHEKER

# The Letter Establishing the Lectureship

Bishop Whitaker presented the Letter of Endowment of the Lectureship on Christian Sociology from Rev. William L. Bull as follows:

For many years it has been my earnest desire to found a Lectureship on Christian Sociology, meaning thereby the application of Christian principles to the Social, Industrial, and Economic problems of the time, in my Alma Mater, the Philadelphia Divinity School. My object in founding this Lectureship is to secure the free, frank, and full consideration of these subjects, with special reference to the Christian aspects of the question involved, which have heretofore, in my opinion, been too much neglected in such discussion. It would seem that the time is now ripe and the moment an auspicious one for the establishment of this Lectureship, at least tentatively.

After a trial of three years, I again make the offer, as in my letter of January 1, 1901, to continue these Lectures for a period of three years, with the hope that they may excite such an interest, particularly among the undergraduates of the Divinity School, that I shall be justified, with the approval of the aut rities of the Divinity School, in placing the Lectureship on a more permanent foundation.

I herewith pledge myself to contribute the sum of six hundred dollars annually, for a period of three years, to the payment of a lecturer on Christian Sociology, whose duty it shall be to deliver a course of not less than four lectures to the students of the Divinity School, either at the school or elsewhere, as may be deemed most advisable, on the application of Christian principles to the Social, Industrial, and Economic problems and needs of the times ; the said lecturer to be appointed annually by a committee of five members : the Bishop of the Diocese of Pennsylvania ; the Dean of the Divinity School ; a member of the Board of Overseers, who shall at the same time be an Alumnus ; and two others, one of whom shall be myself and the other chosen by the preceding four members of the committee.

Furthermore, if it shall be deemed desirable that the Lectures shall be published, I pledge myself to the additional payment of from one to two hundred dollars for such purpose.

To secure a full, frank, and free consideration of the questions involved, it is my desire that the opportunity shall be given from time to time to the representatives of each school of economic thought to express their views in these Lectures.

The only restriction I wish placed on the lecturer is that he shall be a believer in the moral teachings and principles of the Christian Religion as the true solvent of our Social, Industrial, and Economic problems. Of course, it is my intention that a new lecturer shall be appointed by the committee each year, who shall deliver the course of Lectures for the ensuing year.

WILLIAM LEVI BULL.

# Contents

# CHAPTER I

WE are now, I think, far enough removed from the period of slavery to be able to study the influence of that institution objectively rather than subjectively. Surely if any Negro who was a part of the institution itself can do so, the remaining portion of the American people ought to be able to do so, whether they live at the North or at the South.

My subject naturally leads me to a discussion of the Negro as he was in slavery. We must all acknowledge, whatever else resulted from slavery that, first of all, it was the economic element involved that brought the Negro to America, and it was largely this consideration that held the race in slavery for a period of about 245 years.

But, in this discussion, I am not to consider the economic value of the Negro as a slave, as such, but only the influence of his industrial training while in slavery in the development of his moral and religious life.

In my opinion, it requires no little effort on the part of a man who was once himself a slave to be able to admit this. If any Negro who was a part of the institution of slavery itself can so far rid himself of the prejudices of the same, it seems to me other people, living in whatever section, should be able to do so.

I have been a slave once in my life—a slave in body. But I long since resolved that no inducement and no influence would ever make me a slave in soul, in my love for humanity, and in my search for truth.

At the same time slaves were being brought to the shores of Virginia from their native land, Africa, the woods of Virginia were swarming with thousands of another dark-skinned race. The question naturally arises : Why did the importers of Negro slaves go to the trouble and expense of going thousands of miles for a dark-skinned people to hew wood and draw water for the whites, when they had right among them a people of another race who could have answered the purpose? The answer is that the Indian was tried and found wanting in the commercial qualities which the Negro seemed to possess. The Indian, as a race, would not submit to slavery and in those instances where he was tried, as a slave, his labor was not profitable and he was found unable to stand the physical strain of slavery. As a slave, the Indian died in large numbers. This was true in San Domingo and in other parts of the American continent.

The two races, the Indian and the Negro, have been often compared to the disadvantage of the Negro. It is often said of the Negro that he is an imitative race. That, in a large degree, is true. That element has its disadvantages and it also has its advantages. Very often the Negro imitates the worst element in the white man; on the other hand I believe that the masses of our people imitate the best they find in the white man.

I have said more than once that one of the unfortunate conditions of the Negro in the North is that,—because of the large proportion of our people who are in menial service, their duties bring them in contact with the worst. They, for example, are waiters in clubs and in various organizations, and being engaged in that capacity makes it necessary for them to touch the white man at his weakest point. In the city of Philadelphia, there are hundreds, I do not suppose I should exaggerate if I were to say thousands, who are serving the white man as a waiter in some club or similar organization. When that white man was at work in his factory, in his counting-room, in his bank, he was far removed from him. When he was at his best the Negro did not come into touch with him. In the evening when he lays aside the working dress, takes matters easy, and gets his cigar and perhaps champagne, the Negro comes into contact with him, not to an advantage, but at his weakest point rather than at his strongest.

In the South, as in most parts of America, during slavery and after, the Negro has gotten something from the white man that has made him more valuable as a citizen. In most cases he imitates the best rather than the worst. For example, you never see a Negro braiding his hair in the same way as a Chinaman braids his, but he cuts his like the white man. The Negro is seeking out the highest and best as to quality.

It has been more than once stated that the Indian proved himself the superior race in not submitting to slavery. We shall see about this. In this respect it may be that the Indian secured a temporary advantage in so far as race feeling or prejudice is concerned; I mean by this that he escaped the badge of servitude which has fastened itself upon the Negro,—not only upon the Negro in America, but upon that race wherever found, for the known commercial value of the Negro has made him a subject of traffic in other portions of the globe during many centuries.

The Indian refused to submit to bondage and to learn the white man's ways. The result is that the greater portion of the American Indians have disappeared, the greater portion of those who remain are not civilized. The Negro, wiser and more enduring than the Indian, patiently endured slavery; and contact with the white man has given him a civilization vastly superior to that of the Indian.

The Indian and the Negro met on the American continent for the first time at Jamestown, in 1619. Both were in the darkest barbarism. There were twenty

Negroes and thousands of Indians. At the present time there are between nine and ten million Negroes and two hundred and eighty-four thousand and seventy-nine Indians. The annual tax upon the Government on account of the Indian is $14,236,-078.71 (1905); the cost from 1789 to 1902, inclusive, reached the sum of $389,282,-361.00. The one in this case not only decreased in numbers and failed to add anything to the economic value of his country, but has actually proven a charge upon the state.

The Negro seems to be about the only race that has been able to look the white man in the face during the long period of years and live—not only live, but multiply. The Negro has not only done this, but he has had the good sense to get something from the white man at every point where he has touched him—something that has made him a stronger and a better race.

Let me say in the beginning that nothing

which I shall say should be taken as an endorsement of the enslavement of my race. The experience of the world's civilization teaches that the final and net result of slavery is bad—bad for the enslaved, and perhaps worse for the enslaver. If permitted a choice, I think I should prefer being the first to being the last. But in the case of the Negro in America no one, willing to be frank and fair, can fail to see that the Negro did get certain benefits out of slavery ; at the same time he was, as I have stated, harmed. But in this connection we must deal with the facts and not with prejudice, either for or against the race.

Let me make this statement with which you may or may not agree : In my opinion, there cannot be found in the civilized or uncivilized world ten millions of Negroes whose economic, educational, moral and religious life is so advanced as that of the ten millions of Negroes within the United States. If this statement be true, let us find the cause thereof, especially as regards the Negro's moral and Christian growth. In doing so, let credit be given wherever it is due, whether to the Northern white man, the Southern white man, or the Negro himself. If, as stated, the ten millions of black people in the United States have excelled all the other groups of their race-type in moral and Christian growth, let us trace the cause, and in doing so we may get some light and information that will be of value in dealing with the Negro race in America and elsewhere, and in elevating and Christianizing other races.

In order to determine the influence of economic or industrial training upon the moral and Christian life of the Negro, we must begin with slavery and trace the development of the black man, noticing in a brief manner his development through slavery to freedom, and to the present time.

This involves, then, the period of slavery,

and the period of freedom. To begin with, let me repeat that at first, at least, the underlying object of slavery was an economic, and an industrial one. The climatic and other new conditions required that the slave should wear clothing, a thing, for the most part, new to him. It has perhaps already occurred to you that one of the conditions requisite for the Christian life is clothing. So far as I know, Christianity is the only religion that makes the wearing of clothes one of its conditions. A naked Christian is impossible—and I may add that I have little faith in a hungry Christian.

Some years ago we were holding the Tuskeegee Annual Negro Conference, and I remember on several occasions there was one old fellow who tried to get the floor without success. He tried continually to get recognition from the chair, and, finally, was recognized. He said: "Mr. Washington, we's making great progress in our community. It is not the same as it used to be. We's making great progress. We's getting to the point where nearly all the people in my community owns their own pigs." I asked him why he was so much interested in his neighbors owning their own pigs. He said : " I feel that when all my neighbors own their own pigs, I can always sleep better every night." There is a good deal of philosophy underlying that remark.

The economic element not only made it necessary that the Negro slave should be clothed for the sake of decency and in order to preserve his health, but the same considerations made it necessary that he be housed and taught the comforts to be found in a home. Within a few months, then, after the arrival of the Negro in America, he was wearing clothes and living in a house—no inconsiderable step in the direction of morality and Christianity. True, the Negro slave had worn some kind of garment and occupied some kind of hut before he was brought to America, but he had made little progress in the improvement of his garments or in the kind of hut he inhabited. As we shall perhaps see later, his introduction into American slavery was the beginning of real growth in the two directions under consideration.

There is another important element. In his native country, owing to climatic conditions, and also because of his few simple and crude wants, the Negro, before coming to America, had little necessity to labor. You have, perhaps, read the story, that it is said might be true in certain portions of Africa, of how the native simply lies down on his back under a banana-tree and falls asleep with his mouth open. The banana falls into his mouth while he is asleep and when he wakes up he finds that all he has to do is to chew it—he has his meal already served.

Notwithstanding the fact that, in most

cases, the element of compulsion entered into the labor of the slave, and the main object sought was the enrichment of the owner, the American Negro had, under the regime of slavery, his first lesson in anything like continuous, progressive, systematic labor. I have said that two of the signs of Christianity are clothes and houses, and now I add a third, " work."

In the early days of slavery the labor performed by the slave was naturally of a crude and primitive kind. With the growth of civilization came a demand for a higher kind of labor, hence the Negro slave was soon demanded as a skilled laborer, as well as for ordinary farm and common labor. It soon became evident that from an economic point of view it paid to give the Negro just as high a degree of skill as possible—the more skill, the more dollars. When an ordinary slave sold for, say seven hundred dollars, a skilled mechanic would easily bring on the auction block from fourteen hundred to two thousand dollars. It is strangely true that when a black man would bring two thousand dollars a white man would not bring fifty cents.

As the slave grew in the direction of skilled labor, he was given an increased amount of freedom. This was practiced by some owners to such an extent that the skilled mechanic was permitted to "hire" his own time, working where and for whom he pleased, and for what wage, on condition that he pay his owner so much per month or year, as agreed upon. Not a few masters found that this policy paid better than the one of close personal supervision; many female slaves were trained not only in ordinary house duties, but on every large plantation there was at least one high class seamstress.

I have made a search but have not yet been able to find a single case of abuse of confidence, and the policy to which I have referred was practiced very largely in Virginia and especially in West Virginia—the policy of permitting those slaves who were skilled laborers to work for whom they pleased, on condition that they pay their masters a fixed sum each month or each year. I have never yet heard of a single case of failure at the end of the month or at the end of the year to bring and place in his master's hands the stipulated sum of money.

A discussion of this subject calls to mind one of those curious changes in public opinion and custom with regard to races which often occur in the United States. At the period to which I am now referring, a great number of the Negroes in the South were compelled to follow a trade, and they seem to have no difficulty in pursuing trades there to-day. In the North where the agitation for the Negro's freedom began, it is in most cases difficult, and often impossible, for a black man to find an opportunity to work at any kind of skilled labor. I sometimes wonder which man is the greater sinner,—the man who by force compels the Negro to work without pay, or the man who by physical force and through the force of public sentiment prevents the Negro from working for him, when he is ready, willing, and fit to do so.

I do not overstate the matter when I say that I am quite sure that in one county in the South during the days of slavery there were more colored youths being taught trades than there are members of my race now being taught trades in any of the larger cities of the North.

Before I go further, I ought, in justice, to add that as slavery spread and the owners came to know their slaves better, there appeared in nearly every section of the South, especially in Virginia and South Carolina, a considerable number of slave-holders who rose above the mere idea of economic and selfish gain ; and thus, through the medium of slavery, the opportunity to train the

Negro in morality and Christianity presented itself in many sections of the South. During the days of slavery regular religious services were provided for the slaves, the same minister who served the white congregation preached to the blacks. In some of the most aristocratic families, the Negro children were taught in the Sunday-school ; this was true of the Lees and Jacksons of Virginia, and of the family of Bishop Capers and other men of that type in South Carolina.

At the end of the period of slavery, about two hundred and fifty years, the Negro race as a whole had learned, as I have stated, to wear clothes, to live in a home, to work with a reasonable degree of regularity and system, and a few had learned to work with a high degree of skill. Not only this, the race had reached the point where, from speaking scores of dialects, it had learned to speak intelligently the English language. It had also a fair knowledge of American civilization and had changed from a pagan into a Christian race. Further, at the beginning of his freedom, the Negro found himself in possession of—in fact had a monopoly of—the common and skilled labor throughout the South; not only this, but, by reason of the contact of whites and blacks during slavery, the Negro found business and commercial careers open to him at the beginning of his freedom.

Such conditions were unusual in the case of a race that had been occupying so low a place in the civilization of another people. They resulted from the fact that in slavery when the master wanted a pair of shoes made, he went to the Negro shoemaker for those shoes; when he wanted a suit of clothes, he went to the Negro tailor for those clothes; and when he wanted a house built, he consulted the Negro carpenter and mason about the plans and cost—thus the two races learned to do business with each other. It was an easy step from this to a higher plane of business, hence immediately after the war the Negro found that he could become a dry goods merchant, a grocery merchant, start a bank, go into real estate dealing, and secure the trade not only of his own people, but also of the white man, who was glad to do business with him and thought nothing of it.

In my own town of Tuskeegee there is a colored merchant who, not excepting any other merchant, has the largest trade in that county in retail groceries, and in a recent conversation with him he said that for thirty-five years his customers had been among the best white families of the county. More than a dozen times have I met the man who owned this Negro in the days of slavery and he expressed himself as more than pleased that his former slave had attained the honor of being the most successful grocery dealer in the town of Tuskeegee.

You would be surprised, if you were to

inquire into the facts, to know how the Negro has grown in this direction. In the Southern states there are one hundred and fifteen drug stores owned by Negroes. In Anniston, Alabama, there are two large drug stores owned by black people, and in one section a wholesale drug store owned and operated successfully by a black man. The Negro who to-day owns and operates that large wholesale drug store, selling drugs to the white as well as colored retail druggists, was a slave, I think, until he was twelve or fifteen years of age. It is interesting to know that more banks have been organized in the last three years in the state of Mississippi than ever before. There have been ten banks organized since Vardaman became governor of the state.

For the reasons I have mentioned, the Negro in the South has not only found a practically free field in the commercial world, but in the world of skilled labor. Such a field is not open to him in such a degree in any other part of the United States, or perhaps in the world, as is open in the South. All of this has had a tremendously strong bearing in developing the Negro's moral and Christian life.

In proportion to their numbers, I question whether so large a proportion of any other race are members of some Christian Church as is true of the American Negro. In many cases their practical ideas of Christianity are crude, and their daily practice of religion is far from satisfactory; still the foundation is laid, upon which can be builded a rational, practical and helpful Christian life.

Let me illustrate the value of the economic and industrial training of the Negro. If one chooses, let him try this plan which I have tried on a good many occasions. Go into any village or town, North or South, enter their Baptist and Methodist churches —for the most part they belong to the Baptist Church—and ask their pastors to point

out to you the most reliable, progressive and
leading colored man in the community, the
man who is most given to putting his religious teachings into practice in his daily life,
and in a majority of cases one will have
pointed out to him a Negro who learned a
trade or got some special economic training
during the days of slavery,—in all proba-
bility an individual who has become the
owner of a little piece of land, who lives in
his own house.

Now what lessons for the work that is before us can you and I learn from what I
have attempted to say? The lesson suggested in the elevation of the black race in
America will apply with equal force, in my
opinion, to the inculcating of moral and
Christian principles into *any* race, regard-
less of color, that is in the same relative
stage of civilization.    Here let me add that
in all my advocacy of the value of industrial training I have never done so because
my people are black ; I would advocate the

same kind of training for any race that is on the same plane of civilization as our people are found on at the present time.

But as to the lesson which may prove of direct interest, so far as you are concerned. In the old days, the method of converting the heathen to Christianity was very largely abstract. The Bible was, in most cases, the only argument. In the conversion of the heathen to Christianity or in raising the standard of moral and Christian living for any people, I argue that in the use of the economic element and the teaching of the industries we should be guided by the same rules that are now used in the most advanced methods of ordinary school-teaching—that is, to begin with the known and gradually advance to the unknown; we should advance from the concrete to the abstract. In doing this, industrial education, it seems to me, furnishes a tremendously good opportunity.

Let me illustrate: Not long ago a missionary who was going into a foreign field very kindly asked of me advice as to how he should proceed to convert the people to Christianity. I asked him, first, upon what the people depended mostly for a living in the country where he was to labor; he replied that for the most part they were engaged in sheep raising. I said to him at once that if I were going into that country as a missionary, I should begin my efforts by teaching the people to raise more sheep and better sheep. If he could convince them that Christianity could raise more sheep and better sheep than paganism, he would at once get a hold upon their sympathy and confidence in a way he could not do by following more abstract methods of converting them.

The average man can discern more quickly the difference between good sheep and bad sheep, than he can the difference between Unitarianism and Trinitarianism.

If the Christian missionary can gradually

teach the heathen how to build a better
house than he has used, how to make better
clothes, how to grow, prepare and secure
better food for his daily meals, the missionary will have gone a long way, may I repeat, toward securing the confidence of
the heathen and will have laid the foundation in this concrete manner for interesting
the pagan in a higher moral life and in getting him to appreciate the difference between the heathen life and the Christian
life. In teaching the child to read we use
the objective method; in converting the
heathen we should employ the same method
—and this means the economic or industrial method.

Some six years ago a group of Tuskeegee
graduates and former students went to
Africa for the purpose of giving the natives
in a certain territory of West Africa training in methods of raising American cotton.
They did not go there primarily as missionaries, nor was their chief end the conver-

sion of these pagans to Christianity. Naturally, they began their work by training the
natives how to cultivate their land differently, how and when to plant the crop, and
when to harvest it, and gradually taught
them how to use a small hand gin in getting the cotton ready for market.

Largely through the leadership of this
group of Tuskeegee students, there is shipped
from this section of Africa to the Berlin
market each year many bales of cotton.
The natives have learned through the
teaching of these men to grow more cotton
and better cotton. They have learned to
use their time, have learned that by working systematically and regularly they can
increase their income and thus add to their
independence and supply their wants. Not
only this, but in order that these people
might be fitted for continuous and regular
service in the cotton field, their houses have
been improved and the natives have been
taught how to take better care of their

bodies.    In a word, during the years that these Tuskeegee people have been in the community they have improved the entire economic, industrial, and physical life of the people in this immediate territory.

The result is, as one of the men stated on his last visit to Tuskeegee, there is little difficulty now in getting the children of these people to attend Sunday-school and the older people to attend church ; in fact, in a natural, logical manner they seem to have been converted to the idea that the religion practiced by these Tuskeegee men is superior to their own.    They believe this firmly, because they have seen that better results have been produced through the Christian influence of these Tuskeegee men than has been produced when they had no such leadership.    If these Tuskeegee people had gone there as missionaries of the old type and had confined themselves to abstract teachings of the Bible alone, it would have required many years to have brought about the results which have been attained within a few years.

Some time ago in Montgomery, Alabama, there was a church, attended by members of my race, which happened to be located not very far from the residence of a white family. The cook who served in this white family attended this church to which I refer. The members of the church made considerable noise in their singing, shouting, and praying, and after a while the white family grew rather exasperated because of this noise. One Sunday the church services were prolonged until an unusual hour and there was more noise than usual; so the next morning when the cook came, the lady of the house called her into the sitting-room, and said : " Jane, why in the world do you make so much noise in your worship, in your singing, praying, and shouting? Why don't you be orderly, quiet, and systematic in your worship? Why, Jane, in the Bible we read that in the building of Solomon's Temple, no noise pervaded the silence of the builders.   Why can you not worship in the same way?" The old colored woman looked at her mistress for a few moments and said:   "Lordy, missus, you don't know what we's doing; Lordy, missus, you don't know what we's striving at; we's just blasting out de stone for de foundation ob de Temple."   So, my friends, when you hear us laying so much emphasis upon the moral and economic training, upon home-getting and all those things, remember we are simply trying to teach our people to blast out the foundation of the temple in which we are to grow and be useful.

Says the Psalmist:   "O Lord, how manifold are Thy works; in wisdom hast Thou made them all; the earth is full of Thy riches."   I believe that a wise Providence means that we shall use all the material riches of the earth: soil, wood, minerals, stones, water, air, and what not, as a means through which to reach God and glorify Him.

I have thus briefly dealt with the problem of slavery in its relations to the economic and moral growth of my people. Each one of these periods has presented a problem of tremendous importance and seriousness to your race and to my race.

If more attention had been given to the economic and industrial development of Liberia in the early stages of the history of that republic, Liberia would be far in advance of its present condition both in morals and religion, to say nothing of commercial prosperity. In Liberia there is an immense territory rich with resources. Notwithstanding this, there are no improved or advanced methods of agriculture; the soil is scarcely stirred; there are no carts, wagons or other wheeled vehicles, practically no public roads, no bridges, no railroads; the mineral wealth and the timber wealth remain almost untouched;

and I am told on good authority that, in spite of all this wealth right at the very door of these people, even school-teachers and ministers wear clothing manufactured in the United States or in Europe, and eat canned goods that come from Chicago or Germany.

It requires no argument to impress the fact that the most practical missionary work would have been in the direction of teaching these people how to cultivate the soil in the best manner with the very best implements, how to get the wealth out of their forests and water and mines, how to build roads, decent bridges and decent houses; in a word, how to take hold of the material riches with which Providence has blessed the land and turn these riches into moral and religious growth. This, in my opinion, would have represented the very highest kind of missionary work.

I do not grow discouraged or despondent by reason of great and serious problems.

On the contrary, I deem it a privilege to be permitted to live in an age when great, serious, and perplexing problems are to be met and solved. I would not care to live in a period when there was no weak part of the human family to be helped up and no wrongs to be righted. It is only through struggle and the surmounting of difficulties that races, like individuals, are made strong, powerful, and useful.

This is the road the Negro should travel; this is the road, in my opinion, the Negro will travel. I sometimes fear that in our great anxiety to push forward we lay too much stress upon our former condition. We should think less of our former growth and more of the present and of the things which go to retard or hinder that growth. In one of his letters to the Galatians, St. Paul says : " But the fruit of the Spirit is love, joy, peace, long-suffering, gentleness, goodness, faith, meekness, temperance; against such there is no law."

I believe that it is possible for a race, as it is for an individual, to learn to live up in such a high atmosphere that there is no human law that can prevail against it. There is no man who can pass a law to affect the Negro in relation to his singing, his peace, and his self-control. Wherever I go I would enter St. Paul's atmosphere and, living through and in that spirit, we will grow and make progress and, notwithstanding discouragements and mistakes, we will become an increasingly strong part of the Christian citizenship of this republic.

# CHAPTER II

## THE ECONOMIC DEVELOPMENT OF THE NEGRO RACE SINCE ITS EMANCIPATION

# CHAPTER II

IN the preceding chapter, I referred to
some of the things which the Negro brought
with him out of slavery into his life of freedom that he used to his advantage. I shall
now discuss those things that were to his
disadvantage.

We must bear in mind that one of the in-
fluences of slavery was to impress upon
both master and slave the fact that labor
with the hand was not dignified, was disgraceful, that labor of this character was
something to be escaped, to be gotten rid of
just as soon as possible. Hence, it was very
natural that the Negro race looked forward
to the day of freedom as being that period
when it would be delivered from all necessity of laboring with the hand. It was

natural that a large proportion of the race, immediately after its freedom, should make the mistake of confusing freedom with license. Under the circumstances, any other race would have acted in the same manner.

One of the first and most important lessons, then, to be taught the Negro when he became free was the one that labor with the hand or with the head, so far from being something to be dreaded and shunned, was something that was dignified and something that should be sought, loved, and appreciated. Here began the function of the industrial school for the education of the Negro. This was the uppermost idea of General Armstrong, the father of industrial education of the Negro. And permit me to say right here, that, in my opinion, General Armstrong, more than any other single individual, is the father of industrial education not only for the Negro, but in a large measure for the entire United States. For you must always bear in mind that, prior to the establishment of such institutions as the Hampton Institute, there was practically no systematic industrial training given for either black or white people, either North or South. At the present time more attention is being paid to this kind of education for white boys and girls than is being given to black boys and girls.

It is an interesting thought that this kind of education, started thirty-five years ago for the education of the Negro, has spread throughout the United States, in the North and West, and has taken hold upon the people who once enslaved the Negro in our Southern states.

When industrial schools were first established in the South for the education of members of my race, stubborn objection was raised against them on the part of black people. This was the experience of Hampton, and this in later years was the experience of the Tuskeegee Institute.

I remember that for a number of years after the founding of the Tuskeegee Institute, objection on the part of parents and on the part of students poured in upon me from day to day. The parents said that they wanted their children taught " the book," but they did not want them taught anything concerning farming or household duties. It was curious to note how most of the people worshiped " the book." The parent did not care what was inside the book ; the harder and the longer the name of it, the better it satisfied the parent every time, and the more books you could require the child to purchase, the better teacher you were. His reputation as a first-class pedagogue was added to very largely in that section if the teacher required the child to buy a long string of books each year and each month. I found some white people who had the same idea.

They reminded me further that the Negro for two hundred and fifty years as a slave had been worked, and now that the race was free they contended that their children ought not to be taught to work and especially while in school. In answer to these objections I said to them that it was true that the race had been worked in slavery, but the great lesson which we wanted to learn in freedom was to work. I explained to them that there was a vast difference between being worked and working. I said to them that being worked meant degradation, that working meant civilization.

We have gone on at Tuskeegee from that day until this, emphasizing the difference between being worked and working, until, I am glad to say, every sign of opposition against any form of industrial education has completely disappeared from among parents and students; and I but state the truth when I say that industrial education, whether on the farm or in the carpenter shop or in the cooking class, is even more sought after at Tuskeegee than is training in

purely academic branches. It has been ten
years since I have had a single application
for other than a form of industrial training.
On the contrary, this kind of training is so
popular among them that we have many
applications from other students who live
in other states who wish to devote themselves wholly to the industrial side of education.

From Hampton and Tuskeegee and other
large educational centres the idea of industrial education has spread throughout
the South, and there are now scores of institutions that are giving this kind of training in a most effective and helpful manner ;
so that, in my opinion, the greatest thing
that we have accomplished for the Negro
race within the last twenty-five years has
been to rid his mind of all idea of labor's
being degrading. This has been no inconsiderable achievement. If I were asked to
point out the greatest change accomplished
for the Negro race, I would say that it was

not a tangible, physical change, but a change of the spirit,—the new idea of our people with respect to Negro labor.

Industrial education has had another value wherever it has been put into practice, that is in starting the Negro off in his new life in a natural, logical, sensible manner instead of allowing him to be led into temptation to begin life in an artificial atmosphere without any real foundation.

All races that have reached success and have influenced the world for righteousness have laid their foundation at one stage of their career in the intelligent and successful cultivation of the soil; that is, have begun their free life by coming into contact with earth and wood and stone and minerals. Any people that begins on a natural foundation of this kind, rises slowly but naturally and gradually in the world.

In my work at Tuskeegee and in what I have endeavored to accomplish in writing and in speaking before the public, I have always found it important to stick to nature as closely as possible, and the same policy should be followed with a race. If you will excuse my making a personal reference, just as often as I can when I am at home, I like to get my hoe and dig in my garden, to come into contact with real earth, or to touch my pigs and fowls. Whenever I want new material for an address or a magazine article, I follow the plan of getting away from the town with its artificial surroundings and getting back into the country, where I can sleep in a log cabin and eat the food of the farmer, go among the people at work on the plantations and hear them tell their experiences. I have gotten more material in this way than I have by reading books.

Many of these seemingly ignorant people, while not educated in the way that we consider education, have in reality a very high form of education—that which they have gotten out of contact with nature. Only a few days ago I heard one of these old farmers, who could neither read nor write, give a lesson before a Farmers' Institute that I shall never forget. The old man got up on the platform and began with this remark : " I'se had no chance to study science, but I'se been making some science for myself," and then he held up before the audience a stalk of cotton with only two bolls on it. He said he began his scientific work with that stalk. Then he held up a second stalk and showed how the following year he had improved the soil so that the stalk contained four bolls, and then he held up a third stalk and showed how he had improved the soil and method of cultivation until the stalk contained six bolls, and so he went through the whole process until he had demonstrated to his fellow farmers how he had made a single stalk of cotton pro-duce twelve or fourteen bolls. At the close of the old man's address somebody in the audience asked what his name was. He replied, " When I didn't own no home and was in debt, they used to call me old Jim Hill, but now that I own a home and am out of debt, they call me ' Mr. James Hill.' "

In the previous chapter I referred to the practical benefit that could be achieved in foreign mission fields through economic and industrial development. Now that industrial education is understood and appreciated by the Negro in America, the question which has the most practical value to you and to me is what effect has this kind of development had upon the moral and religious life of the Negro right here in America since the race became free.

By reason of the difficulty in getting reliable and comprehensive statistics, it is not easy to answer this question with satisfaction, but I believe that enough facts can be given to show that economic and industrial development has wonderfully improved the moral and religious life of the Negro race in

America, and that, just in proportion as any race progresses in this same direction, its moral and religious life will be strengthened and made more practical.

Let me first emphasize the fact that in order for the moral and religious life to be strengthened we must of necessity have industry, but along with industry there must be intelligence and refinement. Without these two elements combined, the moral and religious lives of the people are not very much helped.

A few months ago I was in a mining camp composed largely of members of my race who were, for the most part, ignorant and uncultivated, who had had little opportunities in the way of education, but they had been taught to mine coal. The operators of this mine complained that, notwithstanding the unusually high wages being paid during that season, these miners could not be induced to work more than three or four days out of six. The difficulty was right here; these miners were so ignorant that they had few wants, and these were simple and crude. Their wants could be satisfied by working a few days out of each week, and when they had satisfied their wants they could not understand why it was necessary to work any longer, and we must all acknowledge that there is a good deal of human nature in this point of view.

In a case of this kind, what is needed is not only to have the individual educated in industry but to have his hand so trained that he will become ambitious; as one man put it not long ago, "He will want more wants." We should get the man to the point where he will want a house, where his wife will want carpet for the floor, pictures for the walls, books, a newspaper and a substantial kind of furniture. We should get the family to the point where it will want money to educate its children, to support the minister and the church. Later, we should get this family to the point where it will want to put money in the bank and perhaps have the experience of placing a mortgage on some property. When this stage of development has been reached, there is no difficulty in getting individuals to work six days during the week.

I have in mind now an old colored man who lived some four miles from the Institution. I first noticed him a number of years ago as I took my daily exercise after my day's work. I found him and his wife living in a little broken-down cabin and resolved to try an experiment on them to see if I could not get them to realize that that kind of life proved of no benefit. When I began, their wants were for the bare necessities of life only. I gradually began to talk to his wife and urge her to see the importance of living a different kind of life. Without the old man's knowing it, I took pains to tell her of how some of their neighbors were living and about some of the things her neighbors were owning. Some had two-room houses, glass windows, new furniture, and little pieces of carpet, and had whitewashed their houses. Finally she became quite interested.

When I began with the man he was working about three days in the week. The old fellow grew interested and began to work a little longer, until the last time I rode by that house the old man was working nearly every day in the week, while they were living in a two-room house and everything had changed. The hardest task I had was to get him to put up a chimney for the second room, finally he put up one and although it was a pretty rickety, crooked affair, yet it answered the purpose and he felt proud of it. When I left this time he informed me that by the time I came back he would try to have both of those rooms whitewashed. I am not through with that family yet. I am going to work on that woman until through her I will get the old man to work five and six days out of the week.

It should always be borne in mind that, for any person of any race, literary education alone increases his want ; and, if you increase these wants without at the same time training the individual in a manner to enable him to supply these increased wants, you have not always strengthened his moral and religious basis.

The same principle might be illustrated in connection with South Africa. In that country there are six millions of Negroes. Notwithstanding this fact, South Africa suffers to-day perhaps as never before for lack of labor. The natives have never been educated by contact with the white man in the same way as has been true of the American Negro. They have never been educated in the day school nor in the Sunday-school nor in the church, nor in the industrial school or college ; hence their ambitions have never been awakened, their wants have not been increased, and they work perhaps two days out of the week and are in idleness during the remaining portion of the time. This view of the case I had confirmed in a conversation with a gentleman who had large interests in South Africa.

How different in the Southern part of the United States where we have eight millions of black people ! Ask any man who has had practical experience in using the masses of these people as laborers and he will tell you that in proportion to their progress in the civilization of the world, it is difficult to find any set of men who will labor in a more satisfactory way. True, these people have not by any means reached perfection in this regard, but they have advanced on the whole much beyond the condition of the South Africans. The trained American Negro has learned to want the highest and best in our civilization, and as we go on giving him more education, increasing his industrial efficiency and his love of labor,

**he** will soon get to the point where he will work six days out of each week.

But as to the results of industrial training. Following the example of the modern pedagogue, let me begin with that which I know most about, the Tuskeegee Institute. This institution employs one of its officers who spends a large part of his time in keeping in close contact with our graduates and former students. He visits them in their homes and in their places of employment and not only sees for himself what they are doing, but gets the testimony of their neighbors and employers, and I can state positively that not ten per cent of the men and women who have graduated from the Tuskeegee Institute or who have been there long enough to understand the spirit and methods of that institution can be found today in idleness in any part of the country. They are at work because they have learned the dignity and beauty and civilizing influence and, I might add, Christianizing power of labor; they have learned the degradation and demoralizing influence of idleness; they have learned to love labor for its own sake and are miserable unless they are at work. I consider labor one of the greatest boons which our Creator has conferred upon human beings.

Further, after making careful investigation, I am prepared to say that there is not a single man or woman who holds a diploma from the Tuskeegee Institute who can be found within the walls of any penitentiary in the United States.

I have learned that not more than a score of the graduates of the fifteen oldest and largest colleges and industrial schools in the entire South have been sent to prison since these institutions were established. Those who are guilty of crime for the most part are individuals who are without education, without a trade, who own no land, who are not taxpayers, who have no bank account, and who have made no progress in industrial and economic development.

The following extracts from a letter written by a Southern white man to the *Daily Advertiser*, of Montgomery, Alabama, contains most valuable testimony. The letter refers to convicts in Alabama, most of whom are colored :

"I was conversing not long ago with the warden of one of our mining prisons, containing about 500 convicts. The warden is a practical man, who has been in charge of prisoners for more than fifteen years, and has no theories of any kind to support. I remarked to him that I wanted some information as to the effect of manual training in preventing criminality, and asked him to state what per cent. of the prisoners under his charge had received any manual training, besides acquaintance with the crudest agricultural labor. He replied : 'Perhaps about one per cent.' He added : 'No, much less than that. We have here at present only one mechanic ; that is, there is one man who claims to be a house painter.'

" ' Have you any shoemakers ? '

" ' Never had a shoemaker.'

" ' Have you any tailors ? '

" ' Never had a tailor.'

" ' Any printers ? '

" ' Never had a printer.'

" ' Any carpenters ? '

" ' Never had a carpenter. There is not a man in this prison that could saw to a straight line.' "

Now these facts seem to show that manual training is almost as good a preventative of criminality as vaccination is of smallpox.

The records of the South show that ninety per cent. of the colored people in prisons are without knowledge of trades, and sixty-one per cent. are illiterate.

There are few higher authorities on the progress of the Negro than Joel Chandler Harris, of the *Atlanta Constitution*, of " Uncle Remus " fame. Mr. Harris had opportunity to know the Negro before the war, and he has followed his progress closely in freedom.

In a printed statement made some time ago Mr. Harris says:

" The point I desire to make is that the overwhelming majority of the Negroes in all parts of the South, especially in the agricultural regions, are leading sober and industrious lives.   A temperate race is bound to be industrious, and the Negroes are temperate when compared with the whites.   Even in the towns the majority of them are sober and industrious."

Dr. Frissell makes the same statement regarding Hampton Institute.   Not more than a score of the graduates have been sent to prison since these institutions were established.   The majority is among those who are without training and who have made no progress in industrial and economic development.   The idle and criminal classes among them make a great show in the police court records, but right here in Atlanta the respectable and decent Negroes far outnumber those who are on the lists

of the police as old or new offenders. I
am bound to conclude from what I see all
about me, and what I know of the race elsewhere, that the Negro, notwithstanding the
late start he has made in civilization and
enlightenment, is capable of making himself
a useful member in the communities in
which he lives and moves, and that he is
become more and more desirous of conform-
ing to all the laws that have been enacted
for the protection of society.

Some time ago I sent out letters to representative Southern men, covering each ex-
slave state, asking them to state, judging by
their observation in their own communities,
what effect industrial education has upon
the morals and religion of the Negro. To
these questions I received 136 replies as
follows :

Has education improved the morals of the
black race ?

Answers—Yes, 97 ; No, 20 ; Unanswered,
**19.**

Has it made his religion less emotional and more practical?

Answers—Yes, 101; No, 16; Unanswered, 19.

Is it, as a rule, the ignorant or the educated who commit crime?

Answers—Ignorant, 115; Educated, 3; Unanswered, 18.

Does crime grow less as education increases among the colored people?

Answers—Yes, 102; No, 19; Unanswered, 15.

Do not these figures speak for themselves?

If possible I want to give you an idea of the progress of the Negro race in a single county in one of the Southern States. For this purpose I select Gloucester County, Virginia. I take this one for the reason that I had the privilege of visiting it a number of years ago, just about the time when interest in the education of the colored people was beginning to be aroused, and for the further reason that this is one of the counties in Virginia and the South that has been longest under the influence of graduates of the Hampton Institute, or of men and women trained in other centres of education.

Gloucester County is the tide-water section of Eastern Virginia. According to the census of 1890, Gloucester County contained a total population of 12,832, a little over one-half being colored, and both sets of schools are in session from five and a half to six months, and the pay of the two sets of teachers is about the same. The majority of the colored teachers in this county were trained at Hampton, and have been teaching in this county a number of years. For the most part, the teachers of Gloucester County are not mentally superior, but what they lack in methods of teaching and mental alertness is more than made up for by the moral earnestness and the example they set. Most of the teachers are natives of the county, and, what is more important, most of them own property in the county.

Now, what is the economic or material result in one county where the Negro has been given a reasonable chance to make progress? I say "reasonable" because it must be kept in mind that the great body of white people in America, with whom the Negro is constantly compared, have schools that are in session from eight to nine months in the year. Note especially what I am going to say now. According to the public records, the total assessed value of the land in Gloucester County is $666,132.33. Of the total value of the land, the colored people own $87,953.55. The buildings in the county have an assessed valuation of $466,127.05. The colored people pay taxes upon $79,387.00 of this amount. To state it differently, the Negroes of Gloucester County, beginning about forty years ago in poverty, have reached the point where they now own and pay taxes upon one-sixth of the real estate in this county. This property is very largely in the shape of small farms, varying in size from ten to one hundred acres. A large proportion of the farms contain about ten acres.

It is interesting to note the influence of this material growth upon the home life of the people. It is stated upon good authority that about twenty-five years ago at least three-fourths of the colored people lived in one-roomed cabins. Let a single illustration tell the story of the growth. In a school where there were thirty pupils ten testified that they lived in houses containing six rooms, and only one said that he lived in a house containing but a single room.

I repeat, I have always believed that in proportion as the industrial, not omitting the intellectual, condition of my race is improved, in the same degree would their moral and religious life improve.

Some years ago, before the home life and

economic condition of the people had improved, bastardy was common in Gloucester County. In 1903 there were only eight cases of bastardy reported in the whole county, and two of those were among the white population. During the year 1904 there was only one case of bastardy within a radius of ten miles of the court house. Another gratifying evidence of progress is shown by the fact that there is very little evidence of immoral relations existing between the races. In the whole county, during the year 1903, about twenty-five years after the work of education had gotten under way, there were only thirty arrests for misdemeanors; of these sixteen were white, fourteen colored. In 1904 there were fifteen such arrests— fourteen white and one colored. In 1904 there were but seven arrests for felonies; of these two were white and five were colored.

In one point at least the colored people in Gloucester County have set an example

for the rest of the religious world that
ought to receive attention. It is in this
regard : there is only one religious denomi-
nation in all of this county, and that is the
Baptist. No over-multiplying, no over-
lapping, no denominational wrangling and
wasting of money and energy.

My I add that, out of my own observation and experience in the heart of the
South during the last twenty-five years, I
have learned that the man of my race who
has some regular occupation, who owns his
farm, is a taxpayer and perhaps has a little
money in the bank, is the most reliable and
helpful man in the Sunday-school, in the
church, and in all religious endeavor. The
man who has gotten upon his feet in these
directions is almost never charged with
crime, but is the one who has the respect
and the confidence of both races in his
community.

I can give you no better idea of the tremendous advance which the Negro has

made since he became free than to say that largely through the influence of industrial education the race has acquired ownership in land that is equal in area to the combined countries of Belgium and Holland. This, for a race starting in poverty and ignorance forty years ago, it seems to me is a pretty good record.

I would not have you understand that I emphasize material possessions as the chief thing in life or as an object within itself. I emphasize economic growth because the civilization of the world teaches that the possession of a certain amount of material wealth indicates the ability of a race to exercise self-control, to plan to-day for to-morrow, to do without to-day in order that it may possess to-morrow. In other words, a race, like an individual, becomes highly civilized and useful in proportion as it learns to use the good things of this earth, not as an end, but as a means toward promoting its own moral and religious growth and the prosperity and happiness of the world. This is what I advocate for my race; it is what I would advocate for any race.

The average white man of America, in passing judgment upon the black race, very often overlooks the fact that geographically and physically the semi-barbarous Negro race has been thrown right down in the centre of the highest civilization that the world knows anything about. Consciously or unconsciously, you compare the Negro's progress with your progress, forgetting, when you are doing it, that you are placing a pretty severe test on the members of my race. If, for example, we were compared with the civilization of the Oriental countries, the test would not be so severe. But we have been placed in the midst of a pushing, surging, restless, conquering, successful civilization, and you must acknowledge that when the American white man wants to lead, no other race can go far ahead. In fact, he would have the whole field to himself. The progress of the Negro will be in proportion as they learn to get the material things of this world, consecrate them, and weave them into the service of our Heavenly Father.

In conclusion, may I say that I hope the people of this country, North and South, will learn to pray more and more; and, as they pray, to put their hands upon their hearts and then ask God if they were placed in the Negro's state, how, under the circumstances, would they like to be treated by their fellows. Conscience will answer the question.

# CHAPTER III

## THE ECONOMIC REVOLUTION IN THE SOUTH

# CHAPTER III

Two questions may be asked of any group of human beings : first, How do they earn their living, and secondly, What is their attitude toward life?   The first relates to the economic history and condition of that people ; the second is a study of their religion. In these two essays I am to treat the first of these questions under the subject: The Economic Revolution in the South, and the second under the subject :   Christianity in the South.

The last century was notable because of the great change in method and organization of human work and we call the early part of the nineteenth century the time of economic revolution in Europe and to some extent in America.  The southern United States, however, while profoundly influenced by this revolution from the first, has not until to-day actually felt its full effect. The new factory system of the early nineteenth century is just to-day appearing in the South, and yet its appearance in England and New England seventy-five years ago made the South a part of the world industrial organization by making it the seat of cotton culture (see Note 1).

Two diverse developments resulted : In England and the North came a change from household industry to social industry, a step forward which led to an era of machinery, to a curious concentration of individuals and wealth and the necessities of living in certain great centres. That very concentration led to a wonderful contact of man with man which sharpened mind and sharpened thought and in the long run made the Europe of to-day. On the other hand, the southern United States, though really a part of this great system through its work of furnishing raw cotton, did not come into the whirl of the new industry because she had an industrial system which forbade machinery, discouraged human contact, and shackled thought.

Why did this system of slavery persist so long in the South as to be caught in the vortex of the new industrial movement and rendered almost inextricable?

If the South had been a place of intelligent farmers on small farms, we could imagine a development which would have been the wonder of the world ; but because the fathers of the United States were so busy with large questions that they forgot larger ones, so busy settling matters of commerce and representation and politics that they forgot matters of work and justice and human rights—because of this we have in the South one of those curious back eddies of human progress that twist and puzzle advance and thought.

The very forward forces of industry that fastened slavery on the South were weaving a social system which made the enslavement of laborers impossible and unprofitable.  Consequently at the very time when the South ought to have been increasing in intelligence, law and order, the use of machinery, industrial concentration, and the intensive culture of land with the rest of the world, she lost a half century in a development backward toward a dispersing of population, extensive rather than intensive land culture, increased and compulsory ignorance of the laboring class, and the rearing of a complete system of caste and aristocracy (see Note 2).

Evils there were to be sure in the new factory system of Europe and the North, evils which southern leaders did not fail to note and gloat over, but they were evils of another and newer industrial era, which did not stop progress, but gave it added incentive.

The industrial back-set of the South meant of course but one thing: the discovery of the paradox of slavery, the turning from the mistake, and the adoption of remedial measures which should usher into the South the same industrial revolution in methods of work which Europe saw begin a century ago.   This is exactly what has happened, and to-day the Industrial Revolution is beginning south of Mason and Dixon's line.   The forecast of change was apparent by 1850.   Slavery still paid then— was still an economic success, but only under conditions which became more and more impossible of realization because of the factory system and the new industrial conditions in the rest of the world (see Note 3).

It was, in other words, an attempt at an industrial system with the lowest wages, the most oppressive labor laws, and the best natural advantages.   Such a system at such a time carried its own sentence of death : fertile land was becoming scarce in the forties, the horrors of the slave trade had shocked even the eighteenth century, and

southern labor laws which made knowledge
a crime and migration of laborers a capital
offense, simply could not be enforced. It
was in vain that the solidly united capitalistic classes of the South threw themselves
bodily into the fray—raped Mexico, filibus-
tered in Cuba and Central America, en-
couraged slave-smuggling (see Note 4), and
bullied the hesitating North ; their economic
doom was written even if militant Aboli-
tionism had not appeared.

The economic student could have fore-
told and did foretell easily in the forties
and fifties that slavery in the South was
doomed (see Note 5) : even if all available
territory had been thrown wide to the slave
system, slavery could not possibly have
stayed in Kansas and Utah, in New Mexico
or in Arizona ; it could have stayed only
temporarily in Missouri and in Texas. It
had already reached its territorial limit, it
was bound to have evolved something different. It will always be an interesting

speculation as to how soon this economic necessity would have been recognized; whether the South would have had the acumen eventually to see the end, and what sort of gradual change could have come about, had it not been for the political crisis precipitated in 1861.

Then came the war—that disgraceful episode of civil strife when, leaving the arguments of men, the nation appealed to the last resort of dogs, murdering and ravishing each other for four long shameful years (see Note 6).

When this nightmare had passed there came, after the resulting period of disorder, a new régime, a new problem of labor, a new industrial order. Not only that, but gradually in the decade 1870–1880 there were added to the South four new economic activities: first, the iron industry; second, the manufacture of cotton cloth; third, the transportation of these goods to, from, and through the South; and fourth, the general exchange of goods in this growing Southern industrial population—in other words, the Industrial Revolution was beginning in the South. So that the South of the 80's was a different South from the South of the 60's, not simply by reason of emancipation but by reason of new economic possibilities.

However, this change could not go on unhindered by the mistakes of the past. With all that was new in the South, there was also much that was old, and of these old things the most important were the Ideals which slavery handed down—ideals of government, of labor, of caste.

Consequently when the South tried to use its new freed labor on its new industrial possibilities, it went to the problem full of the ideals of slavery, and it made four separate attempts. In the first place it was perfectly natural for a land which had said for generations that free Negro labor was an impossibility, and free Negro citizens unthinkable, to cherish a very distinct idea that the way to get along with the emancipated Negro was to make him a slave in fact if not in name. The idea that was back of the first apprentice laws and the various labor codes passed directly after Lee's surrender was that the labor of the blacks belonged to the former white owners by right and could be directed only by force under a nominal wage system. These labor codes therefore attempted to reestablish slavery without a slave trade (see Note 7).

These ill-advised attempts were frustrated by the Fifteenth Amendment which made the freedmen voters. The Thirteenth Amendment did not abolish slavery—it directed its abolition and the answer to it was the labor codes. The Fourteenth Amendment gave the freedmen civil rights and put a premium on granting them political rights, but the premium was not accepted and the civil rights remained unenforced. The Fifteenth Amendment went to

the root of the matter by putting local political power into the hands of the freedmen
and their friends and this made slavery and
the slave system impossible.

What the nation had before it then was
not the nice academic question as to whether
it would be better to have as voters men of
intelligence or men of ignorance, whether it
would be better to throw into the electorate
of a great modern country a mass of slaves
or a mass of college graduates—no such
question came before the country ; it was, as
we are fond of saying, a situation and not a
theory that confronted the country and that
situation was this : here in the South we
had attempted to abolish slavery by act of
legislature—it was not abolished.   The people who hitherto held power did not believe
in its real abolishment ; a great and growing economic revolution fronted them, cotton was still king.   They were about to
solve that problem—to meet the Revolution—according to their former labor ideals.

One could not expect any other outcome. One could not in justice ask them voluntarily to accept free black labor; the only possible way to insure the solving of that economic problem with labor really free was to put in the South a political power which should make slavery in fact or inference forever impossible. This truth the great Thaddeus Stephens saw, and with a statesmanship far greater than Lincoln's he forced Negro suffrage on the South.

Although the new voters thus introduced in the South were crude and ignorant, and in many ways ill-fitted to rule, nevertheless in the fundamental postulates of American freedom and democracy they were sane and sound. Some of them were silly, some were ignorant, and some were venal, but they were not as silly as those who had fostered slavery in the South, nor as ignorant as those who were determined to perpetuate it, and the black voters of South Carolina never stole half as much as the white voters of Pennsylvania are stealing to-day.

The eternal monument to these maligned victims of a nation's wrong is the fact that they began the abolition of slavery in fact and not merely attack it in theory, they established free schools, and they passed laws on all subjects under which the white South is still content to live (see Note 8). If these men had been protected in their legal rights by the strong arm of the government, they would have been able to protect themselves in a generation or so. They would have increased in intelligence, responsibility, and power, and this the South was determined to prevent. The North wavered ; having put its hand to the plow it looked back, and gradually allowed the black peasantry of the South to be almost completely disfranchised. What happened ?

The time had passed for a reëstablishment of slavery, but serfdom and peonage were still possible and probable. When you have the leading classes of a country with the ideal of slavery in their minds and the laboring classes ignorant and without political power, there is but one system that can ensue and that is serfdom, and through serfdom was the second way in which the South strove to meet its great post-bellum economic problem.

Given these premises the economic answer of the South was, from a business standpoint, perfectly sound. The men who, starting poor after a miserable war, went into the development of the South, went in to make money—to use the great American thesis, they were " not in business for their health." They were going to grant to the laborer just as little as they must ; the laborer was unused to a system of free labor, he was not a steady workman, he was not a skilled workman, he had been for two or three hundred years driven to his work, he took no pride in his work—how could he take pride in that which hitherto had been the badge of his shame?

Now it was not considered the business of the new Southern business man to develop and train the working man. It was his business, as I have said, from the American point of view, to make money. And the consequence was that he evolved a peculiarly ingenious system of land serfdom, which bears many likenesses to the serfdom that replaced slavery in Europe. The land belonged to the landlord—it was rented out to the serf; the serf was nominally free, but as a matter of fact he was not free at all; he was held to his labor: he rose with the morning work bell of slavery days, he was driven to his labor by mounted riders, he was whipped for delinquencies, he received no stipulated return, but on the contrary the owner of the land made the contract, kept the accounts, and gave him enough once or twice a year to make him not too dissatisfied.

After a time this changed somewhat; instead of the land owner himself undertaking the advancing of supplies, a third party, the merchant with capital, came in. In order to enforce such a system it needed to be backed by a peculiar law system—therefore the business men went into politics in the South with the same result as when business men go into politics in the North. Things were done quickly and quietly; they were done not for the good of people who had no political voice, but for the good of those who wielded the political power, *i. e.*, the business men and land owners. The laws were made to favor the landlord and the merchant and to make it easy to exploit the tenant and laborer.

This system, which still is the rule of agricultural labor in the black belt of the South, is not a system of free labor; it is

simply a form of peonage. The black peon
is held down by perpetual debt or petty
criminal judgments; his rent rises with the
price of cotton, his chances to buy land are
either non-existent or confined to infertile
regions. Judge and jury are in honor
bound to hold him down; if by accident or
miracle he escapes and becomes a land-
holder, his property, civil and political
status are still at the mercy of the worst of
the white voters, and his very life at the whim
of the mob. The power of the individual
white patron to protect colored men is still
great and is often exercised, but this is but
another argument against the system: it is
undemocratic and un-American, and stamps
on the serf system its most damning criti-
cism.

Moreover, this second attempt to meet
the economic revolution of the South is
failing, and its failure is shown by the
scarcity of farm labor, the migration of Negroes, and the increase of crime and law-

lessness.   Serfdom like slavery demands ignorance and strict laws.   The decade of
Negro voting and Northern benevolence had
however given the Negro schools and aspiration.

What now has been the reaction of this
group on the environment thrown around
it since slavery days ?

The slaves had their select classes in the
house servants and the artisans.   After freedom came, the Negro made four distinct efforts to reach economic safety.   The first
effort was by means of the select house-serv-
ant class ; the second, by means of com-
petitive industry ; the third, by land-owning ; and the fourth, by what I shall call
the group economy.

First, let us look at the effort of the
house servants.   The one person under the
slave régime who came nearest to escaping
from the toils of slavery and the disabilities
of caste was the favorite house servant.
This was because the house servant was

brought into contact with the culture of the
master and the family, because he had often the advantages of town and city life,
was able to gain some smattering of education, and also because he was usually a
blood relative of the master class. These
house servants, therefore, became the
natural leaders of the emancipated race and
the brunt of the burden of reconstruction
fell upon their shoulders. When the history of this period is carefully written it
will show that few men ever made a more
meritorious fight against overwhelming
odds.

Under free competition it would have
been natural for this class of house servants
to enter the economic life of the nation directly. In some cases this happened, especially in the case of the barber and the
caterer. For the most part, however, the
black applicant was refused admittance to
the economic society of the nation. He
held his own in the semi-servile work of

barber until he met the charge of color discrimination in his own race, and the competition of foreigners. The caterer was displaced by palatial hotels in which he could have no part.

On the whole, then, the mass of house servants soon found the doors in their own lines closed in their faces. They could remain good servants but they could not by this means often escape into higher walks of life. The better tenth of them went gradually into professions and thus found economic independence for themselves and their children. The mass of them either remained house servants or turned toward industry.

The second attempt of the freedmen toward economic safety lay in industry. It was a less ambitious effort than that of the house servants, and included larger numbers of men. It was characterized by a large migration to the towns. Here it was that the class of slave artisans made themselves felt in freedom and they were joined by numbers of unskilled workmen, such as steam railway hands, porters, hostlers, etc. This class attracted considerable attention and bore the brunt of the economic battle in competition with white working men. It is a class that is growing and in the future it is going to have a large development. At present, however, its fight is difficult.

The third effort of economic elevation was by land owning. This was the ideal toward which the great mass of black people looked. They at first thought that the government was going to help them, and the government did in a few instances, as when Sherman distributed land in Georgia and the government sold South Carolina lands for taxes. For the most part, however, the Negroes had to buy their own lands which they did in some cases by means of their bounty money for serving in the army or by means of special monies which they

earned as workmen during the war or by
the help of the former masters.  Some too,
by the share tenant system gained enough
to buy land.  In this way about 200,000 to-
day own their farms and thus approximate
economic independence.

The fourth and last effort, which I call
the Group Economy, is of great importance,
but is not very well understood.  It consists of a coöperative arrangement of industry and service in a group which tends
to make the group a closed economic circle,
largely independent of surrounding whites.
This development explains many anomalies
in the situation of the Negro.   Many people
think that the colored barber is disappear-
ing, yet there are more colored barbers in
the United States to-day than ever before,
but a larger number than ever cater to only
colored trade.  The Negro lawyer serves
almost exclusively colored clientage, so that
his existence is half forgotten by the white
world.  The new Negro business men are

not successors of the old. There used to be
Negro business men in Northern cities and
a few even in Southern cities, but they
catered to white trade; the Negro business
man to-day caters to colored trade. So far
has this gone to-day that in every city in
the United States which has considerable
Negro population, the colored group is
serving itself in religion, medical care,
legal advice and often educating its children. In growing degree also it is serving
itself in insurance, houses, books, amuse-
ments.

So extraordinary has been this development that it forms a large and growing part
in the economy of perhaps half the Negroes
of the United States, and in the case of perhaps 100,000 town Negroes, representing at
least 300,000 persons, the group economy
approaches a complete system. To these
we may add the bulk of 200,000 farmers
who own their farms. Thus we have a
group of half a million who are reaching

economic safety by means of group economy (see Note 9).

Here then are the two developments—a determined effort at an established serfdom on the part of landholding capitalists, and a determined effort on the part of freedmen and their sons to attain economic independence.

While both these movements were progressing the full change of the industrial revolution, so long postponed, began to be felt all over the South; the iron and steel industry developed in Alabama and Tennessee, coal mining in Tennessee and West Virginia, and cotton manufacture in Carolina and Georgia; railways were consolidated into systems and extended, commerce was organized and concentrated. The greatest single visible result of this was the growth of cities. Towns of eight thousand and more had a tenth of the white Southerners in 1860; they held a seventh of a much larger population in

1900, while a fifth were in cities and villages. Still more striking was the movement of Negroes ; only four per cent. were in cities before the war, to-day a seventh are there.

The reason for this is clear : the oppression and serfdom of the country, the opportunities of the city. It was in the town and city alone that the emerging classes, outside the landholders, were successful, and even the landholders were helped by the earnings of the city ; the house servants with the upper class of barbers and caterers, the artisans, the day laborers, the professional men, including the best of the teachers, were in the cities, and the new group economy was developed here.

On the other hand one of the inevitable expedients for fastening serfdom on the country Negro was enforced ignorance.

The Negro school system established by the Negro reconstruction governments reached its culmination in the decade 1870-1880. Since then determined effort has been made in the country districts to make the Negro schools less efficient. To-day these schools are worse than they were twenty years ago ; the nominal term is longer and the enrolment larger, but the salaries are so small that only the poorest local talent can teach. There is little supervision, there are few appliances, few schoolhouses and no inspiration. On the other hand the city schools have usually improved. It was natural that the Negro should rush city-ward toward freedom, education, and decent wages.

This migration resulted in two things : in the increase and intensification of the problems of the city, and in redoubled effort to keep the Negro laborer on the plantations.

To take the latter efforts first, we find that the efforts of the landlords to keep Negro labor varied from force to persuasion : force was used by the landlords to the extent of actual peonage, by which Negroes were held on plantations in large numbers ; next to peonage for crime came debt peonage, which used the indebtedness of the Negro tenants to prevent their moving away ; then came the system of labor contracts and the laws making the breaking of a labor contract a crime (see Note 10) ; after that came a crop of vagrancy laws aimed at the idle Negroes in city and town and designed to compel them to work on farms, going so far in several states as to reverse the common law principle and force the person arrested for vagrancy to prove his innocence (see Note 11).

In order that the farm laborers should not be tempted away by higher wages, penalties were laid on " enticing laborers away " and agents were compelled to take out licenses which ran as high as $2,000 for each county in some states (see Note 12). Such laws and their administration required, of course, absolute control of the government and courts. This was secured by manipulation and fraud, while at the same time the landlords of the black belt usually opposed the disfranchisement of Negroes lest such a measure reduce their political influence which was based on the Negro population.

All these measures were measures of force, while nothing was done to attract laborers to the land. The only real attraction of the Negro to the country was landowning. The Negroes had succeeded in buying land : by government gift and bounty money they held about three million acres in 1875, perhaps 8,000,000 in 1890, and 12,000,000 in 1900 ; but distinct efforts appeared here and there to stop their buying land.

There are still vast tracts of land in the South, that anybody, black or white, can buy for little or nothing, simply because it is worth little or nothing. Some time, of course, these lands will become valuable but they are not valuable to-day. Now the Negro cannot invest in this land as a speculation, for he is too poor to wait. He must have land which he knows how to cultivate, which is near a market, and which is so situated as to provide reasonable protection for his family. There are only certain crops which he knows how to cultivate. He cannot be expected to learn quickly to cultivate crops which he was not taught to cultivate in the past. He must be within reach of a market and he must have some community life with his own people and some protection from other people.

All these conditions are fulfilled chiefly in the black belt. That is the cotton region, the crop which he knows best how to raise; from certain parts of it he can get to the market and he has a great black population for company and protection. But it is precisely here in the black belt that it is most difficult to buy land. Capitalistic culture of cotton, the high price of cotton, and the system of labor peonage have made land high.  Moreover in most of these regions it is considered bad policy to sell Negroes land because, as has been said, this " demoralizes " labor.  Thus in the densest part of the black belt in the South, the percentage of land holding is usually low among Negroes.

The concentration of land-owning on the other hand in the hands of the single white proprietors has gone on to a much larger extent than the country realizes.  This is shown not simply in the increase of the average size of farms in the last decade but it must also be remembered that the farms do not belong to single owners but are owned in groups of five, forty or fifty by single landed proprietors.  There are 140,000 owners who own from two to fifty farms in the South and there are 50,000 owners who have over twenty farms apiece.

It is not true then to-day that land-buying for the average colored farmer in the South is an easy thing.  The land which has been bought has been bought by the exceptional men or by the men who have had unusual opportunity, who have been helped by their former masters or by some other patrons, who have been aided by members of their own families in the North or in the cities, or who have escaped the wretched crop system by some sudden rise in the price of cotton, which did not enable the landlord to take the whole economic advantage. It is therefore in spite of the land system and not because of it that the Negroes to-day own 12,000,000 acres of land (see Note 13).

The net result of the whole policy of serfdom was so to deplete the ranks of laborers that a new solution of the labor problem must be found.

Here it was that the southern city came forward. The city had new significance, especially new cities like Atlanta, Birmingham, and Chattanooga as contrasted with Charleston and Savannah. They saw a

new industrial solution of the problem of
Negro labor. It was a simple program :
Industry and disfranchisement ; the separation of the masses of the Negroes from all
participation in government, and such technical training as should fit them to become
skilled working men.

There was an *arriere pensee* here too, born
in the minds of northern capitalists. The
white southern working men were becoming
unionized by northern agitators ; here was a
chance to keep them down to reasonable
demands by black competition and the
threat of more competition in the future.
Moreover working men without votes would
be far more docile and tractable. Politics
had already spoiled the Negroes. Let the
whites rule and the blacks work.

The plea was specious, it had the sanction
of great names, of wealth and social influence, and it convinced not only those
who wanted to be convinced but practically all Americans who were eager to be

relieved of troublesome questions and difficult public duties.

All the more eagerly was this solution seized upon because of the definite and distinct promises which it made. Disfranchise the Negro, said the South, and the race problem is solved; there is no race problem save the menace of an ignorant and venal vote;—relieve us from this and the lion and the lamb will lie down together;—the Negro will go peacefully and contentedly to work and the whites will wax just and rich. We all remember with what confidence and absolute certainty of conviction this program was announced when Mississippi disfranchised her Negro voters seventeen years ago. It was repeated twelve years ago in South Carolina, ten years ago in Louisiana, and still more recently in North Carolina and Alabama.

What has been the result? Is the race problem solved? Is the Negro out of politics in the South? Has there been a single southern campaign in the last twenty years in which the Negro has not figured as the prime issue? Have the southern representatives in Congress any settled convictions or policy save hatred of black men, and can they discuss any other matter? Is it not the irony of fate that in the state that first discovered the legal fraud of disfranchisement a hot political battle is today waging on the old, old question: the right of black men to vote?

The reason for all this is not far to seek. In modern industrial democracy disfranchisement is impossible. The fate, wishes, and destiny of ten million human beings cannot be delivered, sealed and bound into the keeping of Dixon, Tillman, Vardaman, and Nelson Page. They are bound to vote even when disfranchised.

Disfranchised and voiceless though I am in Georgia to-day by the illegal White Primary system, there are still fifty congressmen in Washington fraudulently representing me and my fellows in the councils of the nation (see Note 14).

It was promised that disfranchisement would lead to more careful attention to the Negro's moral and economic advancement. It has on the contrary stripped them naked to their enemies; discriminating laws of all sorts have followed, the administration of other laws has become harsher and more unfair, school funds have been curtailed and education discouraged, and mobs and murder have gone on.

If the new policy has been a farce politically and socially, how much more has it failed as an economic cure-all! No sooner was it proclaimed from the house-tops than the rift in the lute appeared. " We do not want educated farmers," cried the landlords, " we want docile laborers." " We do not want educated Negro artisans," cried the white artisans, and they enforced their demands by their votes and by mob violence. " We do not want to raise the Negro ; we want to put him in his place and keep him there," cried the dominant forces of the South. Then those northerners who had lightly embraced the fair sounding program of limited labor training and disfranchisement found themselves grasping the air.

Not only this, but the South itself faced a puzzling paradox. The industrial revolution was demanding labor; it was demanding intelligent labor, while the supposed political and social exigences of the situation called for ignorance and subserviency. It was an impossible contradiction and the South to-day knows it.

What is it that makes a successful laboring force? It is laborers of education and natural intelligence, reasonably satisfied with their conditions, inspired with certain ideals of life, and with a growing sense of self-respect and self-reliance. How is the caste system of the South influencing the Negro laborer? It is systematically re-

stricting his development; it is restricting
his education so that the public common
schools of the South except in a few cities
are worse this moment than they were
twenty years ago; it is seeking to kill self-
respect by putting upon the accident of
color every mark of humiliation that it can
invent; it is discouraging self-reliance by
treating a class of men as wards and children; it is killing ambition by drawing a
color line instead of a line of desert and ac-
complishment; and finally, through these
things, it is encouraging crime, and by the
unintelligent and brutal treatment of criminals, it is developing more crime.

This general attitude toward the main
laboring class reflects itself less glaringly
but as certainly in the treatment even of
white laborers. So long as white labor
must compete with black labor, it must approximate black labor conditions—long
hours, small wages, child labor, labor of
women, and even peonage. Moreover it

can raise itself above black labor only by a legalized caste system which will cut off competition and this is what the South is straining every nerve to create.

The last fatal campaign in Georgia which culminated in the Atlanta Massacre was an attempt, fathered by conscienceless politicians, to arouse the prejudices of the rank and file of white laborers and farmers against the growing competition of black men, so that black men by law could be forced back to subserviency and serfdom. It succeeded so well that smouldering hate burst into flaming murder before the politicians could curb it.

There is, however, a limit to this sort of thing. The day when mobs can successfully cow the Negro to willing slavery is past. The Atlanta Negroes shot back and shot to kill, and that stopped the riot with a certain suddenness (see Note 15). The South is realizing that lawlessness and economic advance cannot coexist. If the

wonderful industrial revolution is to develop
unhindered, the South must have law and
order and it must have intelligent workmen.

It is only a question of time when white
working men and black working men will
see their common cause against the aggressions of exploiting capitalists.    Already
there are signs of this : white and black
miners are working as a unit in Alabama ;
white and black masons are in one union
in Atlanta (see Note 16).    The economic
strength of the Negro cannot be beaten into
weakness, and therefore it must be taken
into partnership, and this the Southern
white working man, befuddled by prejudice
as he is, begins dimly to realize.

It is this paradox that brings us to-day in
the South to a fourth solution of the problem : Immigration.    The voice that calls
foreign immigrants southward to-day is not
single but double.    First, the exploiter of
common labor wishes to exploit this new
labor just as formerly he exploited Negro

labor. On the other hand the far-sighted ones know that the present freedom of labor exploitation must pass—that some time or other the industrial system of the South must be made to conform more and more to the growing sense of industrial justice in the North and in the civilized world. Consequently the second object of the immigration philosopher is to make sure that, when the rights of the laborer come to be recognized in the South, that laborer will be white, and just so far as possible the black laborer will still be forced down below the white laborer until he becomes thoroughly demoralized or extinct.

The query is therefore : If immigration turns toward the South as it undoubtedly will in time, what will become of the Negro? The view of the white world is usually that there are two possibilities. First, that the immigrants will crush the Negro utterly ; or secondly, that by competition there will come a sifting which will

lead to the survival of the best in both
groups of laborers.

Let us consider these possibilities.  First
it is certain that so far as the Negroes are
land holders, and so far as they belong
to a self-employing, self-supplying group
economy, no possible competition from
without can disturb them.  I have shown
already how rapidly this system is growing.  Further than that, there is a large
group of Negroes who have already gained
an assured place in the national economy
as artisans, servants, and laborers.  The
worst of these may be supplanted, but the
best could not be unless there came a sudden unprecedented and improbable influx
of skilled foreign labor.  A slow infiltration
of foreigners cannot displace the better class
of Negro workers; simply because the growing labor demand of the South cannot spare
them.  If then it is to be merely a matter
of ability to work, the result of immigration
will on the whole be beneficial and will

differentiate the good Negro workman from the careless and indifferent.

But one element remains to be considered, and this is political power. If the black workman is to remain disfranchised while the white native and immigrant not only has the economic defense of the ballot, but the power to use it so as to hem in the Negro competitor, cow and humiliate him and force him to a lower plane, then the Negro will suffer from immigration.

It is becoming distinctly obvious to Negroes that to-day, in modern economic organization, the one thing that is giving the workman a chance is intelligence and political power, and that it is utterly impossible for a moment to suppose that the Negro in the South is going to hold his own in the new competition with immigrants if, on the one hand, the immigrant has access to the best schools of the community and has equal political power with other men to defend his rights and to assert his wishes, while, on the other hand, his black competitor is not only weighed down by past degradation, but has few or no schools and is disfranchised.

The question then as to what will happen in the South when immigration comes, is a very simple question.   If the Negro is kept disfranchised and ignorant and if the new foreign immigrants are allowed access to the schools and given votes as they undoubtedly will be, then there can ensue only accentuated race hatred, the spread of poverty and disease among Negroes, the increase of crime, and the gradual murder of the eight millions of black men who live in the South except in so far as they escape North and bring their problems there as thousands will.

If on the contrary, with the coming of the immigrants to the South, there is given to the Negro equal educational opportunity and the chance to cast his vote like a man and be counted as a man in the councils of the county, city, state and nation, then there will ensue that competition between men in the industrial world which, if it is not altogether just, is at least better than slavery and serfdom.

There of course could be strong argument that the nation owes the Negro something better than harsh industrial competition just after slavery, but the Negro does not ask the payment of debts that are dead. He is perfectly willing to come into competition with immigrants from any part of the world, to welcome them as human beings and as fellows in the struggle for life, to struggle with them and for them and for a greater South and a better nation. But the black man certainly has a right to ask, when he starts into this race, that he be allowed to start with hands untied and brain unclouded (see Note 17).

Such in bare outline is the economic history of the South. It is the story of an attempt to degrade working men. It failed in

1860, after it had sought for centuries to reduce laborers to the level of purchasable
cattle; it failed in 1870, after a fearful
catastrophe while endeavoring to revive
this system under another name; it has
failed since then satisfactorily to maintain
the present rural serfdom or to establish a
disfranchised caste of artisans; and it will
fail in the future to keep the stubbornly
up-struggling masses of black laborers down,
by shackling their souls and loading immigrants atop of them. It will always fail
unless indeed, as sometimes seems possible,
both Church and State in America shall refuse longer to listen to the teaching of Jesus
when He said : " Come unto Me all ye that
labor and are heavy-laden, and I will give
you rest.

"Take My yoke upon you and learn of
Me; for I am meek and lowly in heart : and
ye shall find rest for your souls.

"For My yoke is easy and My burden is
light."

# CHAPTER IV

## RELIGION IN THE SOUTH

# CHAPTER IV

It is often a nice question as to which is of greater importance among a people—the way in which they earn their living, or their attitude toward life. As a matter of fact these two things are but two sides of the same problem, for nothing so reveals the attitude of a people toward life as the manner in which they earn their living; and on the other hand the earning of a living depends in the last analysis upon one's estimate of what life really is. So that these two questions that I am discussing with regard to the South are intimately bound up with each other.

If we have studied the economic development of the South carefully, then we have already seen something of its attitude toward life; the history of religion in the

South means a study of these same facts over which we have gone, from a different point of view. Moreover, as the economic history of the South is in effect the economics of slavery and the Negro problem, so the essence of a study of religion in the South is a study of the ethics of slavery and emancipation.

It is very difficult of course for one who has not seen the practical difficulties that surround a people at any particular time in their battle with the hard facts of this world, to interpret with sympathy their ideals of life; and this is especially difficult when the economic life of a nation has been expressed by such a discredited word as slavery. If, then, we are to study the history of religion in the South, we must first of all divest ourselves of prejudice, pro and con ; we must try to put ourselves in the place of those who are seeking to read the riddle of life and grant to them about the same general charity and the same general desire to do right that we find in the average human being. On the other hand, we must not, in striving to be charitable, be false to truth and right. Slavery in the United States was an economic mistake and a moral crime. This we cannot forget. Yet it had its excuses and mitigations. These we must remember.

When in the seventeenth century there grew up in the New World a system of human slavery, it was not by any means a new thing. There were slaves and slavery in Europe, not, to be sure, to a great extent, but none the less real. The Christian religion, however, had come to regard it as wrong and unjust that those who partook of the privileges and hopes and aspirations of that religion should oppress each other to the extent of actual enslavement. The idea of human brotherhood in the seventeenth century was of a brotherhood of co-religionists. When it came to the dealing of Christian with heathen, however, the century saw nothing wrong in slavery; rather, theoretically, they saw a chance for a great act of humanity and religion. The slaves were to be brought from heathenism to Christianity, and through slavery the benighted Indian and African were to find their passport into the kingdom of God. This theory of human slavery was held by Spaniards, French, and English. It was New England in the early days that put the echo of it in her codes (see Note 18) and recognition of it can be seen in most of the colonies.

But no sooner had people adopted this theory than there came the insistent and perplexing question as to what the status of the heathen slave was to be after he was Christianized and baptized; and even more pressing, what was to be the status of his children?

It took a great deal of bitter heart searching for the conscientious early slave-holders to settle this question. The obvious state of things was that the new convert awoke immediately to the freedom of Christ and became a freeman. But while this was the theoretical, religious answer, and indeed the answer which was given in several instances, the practice soon came into direct and perplexing conflict with the grim facts of economic life.

Here was a man who had invested his money and his labor in slaves ; he had done it with dependence on the institution of property. Could he be deprived of his property simply because his slaves were baptized afterward into a Christian church ? Very soon such economic reasoning swept away the theological dogma and it was expressly declared in colony after colony that baptism did not free the slaves (see Note 19). This, of course, put an end to the old doctrine of the heathen slave and it was necessary for the church to arrange for itself a new theory by which it could ameliorate, if not excuse, the position of the slave. The next question was naturally that of the children of slaves born in Christianity and the church for a time hedged unworthily on the subject by consigning to perpetual slavery the children of heathen but not those born of Christian parents ; this was satisfactory for the first generation but it fell short of the logic of slavery later, and a new adjustment was demanded.

Here again this was not found difficult. In Virginia there had been built up the beginnings of a feudal aristocracy. Men saw nothing wrong or unthinkable in the situation as it began to develop, but rather something familiar. At the head of the feudal manor was the lord, or master, beneath him the under-lord or overseers and then the artisans, retainers, the free working men and lastly the serfs, slaves or servants as they were called. The servant was not free and yet he was not theoretically exactly a slave, and the laws of Virginia were rather careful to speak very little of slaves.

Serfdom in America as in Europe was to be a matter of status or position and not of race or blood, and the law of the South in the seventeenth and early eighteenth centuries made little or no distinction between black and white bondservants save in the time of their service. The idea, felt rather than expressed, was that here in America we were to have a new feudalism suited to the new country. At the top was the governor of the colony representing the majesty of the English king, at the bottom the serfs or slaves, some white, most of them black.

Slavery therefore was gradually transformed in the seventeenth and eighteenth centuries into a social status out of which a man, even a black man, could escape and did escape ; and, no matter what his color was, when he became free, he became free in the same sense that other people were. Thus it was that there were free black voters in the southern colonies (Virginia and the Carolinas) in the early days concerning whose right to vote there was less question than there is concerning my right to vote now in Georgia (see Note 20).

The church recognized the situation and the Episcopal church especially gave itself easily to this new conception. This church recognized the social gradation of men ; all souls were equal in the sight of God, but there were differences in worldly consideration and respect, and consequently it was perfectly natural that there should be an aristocracy at the top and a group of serfs at the bottom.

Meantime, however, America began to be stirred by a new democratic ideal ; there came the reign of that ruler of men, Andrew Jackson ; there came the spread of the democratic churches, Methodist and Baptist, and the democratization of other churches. Now when America became to be looked upon more and more as the dwelling place of free and equal men and when the Methodist and, particularly, the Baptist churches went down into the fields and proselyted among the slaves, a thing which the more aristocratic Episcopal church had never done (see Note 21), there came new questions and new heart-searchings among those who wanted to explain the difficulties and to think and speak clearly in the midst of their religious convictions.

As such people began to look round them the condition of the slaves appalled them. The Presbyterian Synod of South Carolina and Georgia declared in 1833 : " There are over two millions of human beings in the condition of heathen and some of them in a worse condition. They may be justly considered the heathen of this country, and will bear a comparison with heathen in any country in the world. The Negroes are destitute of the gospel, and ever will be under the present state of things. In the vast field extending from an entire state beyond the Potomac [*i. e.*, Maryland] to the

Sabine River [at the time our southwestern boundary] and from the Atlantic to the Ohio, there are, to the best of our knowledge, not twelve men exclusively devoted to the religious instruction of the Negroes. In the present state of feeling in the South, a ministry of their own color could neither be obtained nor tolerated.

"But do not the Negroes have access to the gospel through the stated ministry of the whites? We answer, no. The Negroes have no regular and efficient ministry; as a matter of course, no churches; neither is there sufficient room in the white churches for their accommodation. We know of but five churches in the slave-holding states built expressly for their use. These are all in the state of Georgia. We may now inquire whether they enjoy the privileges of the gospel in their own houses, and on our plantations? Again we return a negative answer. They have no Bibles to read by their own firesides. They have no family

altars; and when in affliction, sickness, or
death, they have no minister to address to
them the consolations of the gospel, nor to
bury them with appropriate services."

The same synod said in 1834: "The
gospel, as things now are, can never be
preached to the two classes (whites and
blacks) successfully in conjunction. The
galleries or back seats on the lower floor of
white churches are generally appropriated
to the Negroes, when it can be done without
inconvenience to the whites. When it cannot be done conveniently, the Negroes must
catch the gospel as it escapes through the
doors and windows. If the master is pious,
the house servants alone attend family
worship, and frequently few of them, while
the field hands have no attention at all.
So far as masters are engaged in the work
[of religious instruction of slaves], an almost unbroken silence reigns on this vast
field."

The Rev. C. C. Jones, a Georgian and

ardent defender of slavery (see Note 22) says of the period 1790–1820: " It is not too much to say that the religious and physical condition of the Negroes were both improved during this period. Their increase was natural and regular, ranging every ten years between thirty-four and thirty-six per cent. As the old stock from Africa died out of the country, the grosser customs, ignorance, and paganism of Africa died with them. Their descendants, the country-born, were better looking, more intelligent, more civilized, more susceptible of religious impressions.

" On the whole, however, but a minority of the Negroes, and that a small one, attended regularly the house of God, and taking them as a class, their religious instruction was extensively and most seriously neglected."

And of the decade 1830–40, he insists: " We cannot cry out against the Papists for withholding the Scriptures from the common people and keeping them in ignorance

of the way of life, for we withhold the Bible
from our servants, and keep them in ignorance of it, while we will not use the
means to have it read and explained to
them."

Such condition stirred the more radical-
minded toward abolition sentiments and
the more conservative toward renewed effort
to evangelize and better the condition of
the slaves.  This condition was deplorable
as Jones pictures it.  " Persons live and die
in the midst of Negroes and know com-
paratively little of their real character.
They have not the immediate management
of them.  They have to do with them in
the ordinary discharge of their duty as
servants, further than this they institute no
inquiries; they give themselves no trouble.

" The Negroes are a distinct class in the
community, and keep themselves very much
to themselves.  They are one thing before
the whites and another before their own
color.  Deception before the former is char-

acteristic of them, whether bond or free, throughout the whole United States. It is habit, a long established custom, which descends from generation to generation. There is an upper and an under current. Some are contented with the appearance on the surface; others dive beneath. Hence the diversity of impressions and represen- tations of the moral and religious condition of the Negroes. Hence the disposition of some to deny the darker pictures of their more searching and knowing friends."

He then enumerates the vice of the slaves : " The divine institution of marriage depends for its perpetuity, sacredness, and value, largely upon the protection given it by the law of the land. Negro marriages are neither recognized nor protected by law. The Negroes receive no instruction on the nature, sacredness, and perpetuity of the institution ; at any rate they are far from being duly impressed with these things. They are not required to be married in any particular form, nor by any particular persons."

He continues : " Hence, as may well be imagined, the marriage relation loses much of the sacredness and perpetuity of its character. It is a contract of convenience, profit, or pleasure, that may be entered into and dissolved at the will of the parties, and that without heinous sin, or the injury of the property or interests of any one. That which they possess in common is speedily divided, and the support of the wife and children falls not upon the husband, but upon the master. Protracted sickness, want of industrial habits, of congeniality of disposition, or disparity of age, are sufficient grounds for a separation."

Under such circumstances, " polygamy is practiced both secretly and openly." Uncleanness, infanticide, theft, lying, quarreling, and fighting are noted, and the words of Charles Cotesworth Pinckney in 1829 are recalled : " There needs no stronger illustration of the doctrine of human depravity than the state of morals on plantations in general. Besides the mischievous tendency of bad example in parents and elders, the little Negro is often taught by these natural instructors that he may commit any vice that he can conceal from his superiors, and thus falsehood and deception are among the earliest lessons they imbibe. Their advance in years is but a progression to the higher grades of iniquity. The violation of the Seventh Commandment is viewed in a more venial light than in fashionable European circles. Their depredations of rice have been estimated to amount to twenty-five per cent. of the gross average of crops."

John Randolph of Roanoke once visited a lady and "found her surrounded with her seamstresses, making up a quantity of clothing. 'What work have you in hand?' 'O sir, I am preparing this clothing to send to the poor Greeks.' On taking leave at the steps of her mansion, he saw some of her servants in need of the very clothing which their tender-hearted mistress was sending abroad. He exclaimed, 'Madam, madam, the Greeks are at your door!'"

One natural solution of this difficulty was to train teachers and preachers for the slaves from among their own number. The old Voodoo priests were passing away and already here and there new spiritual leaders of the Negroes began to arise. Accounts of several of these, taken from "The Negro Church," will be given.

Among the earliest was Harry Hosier who traveled with the Methodist Bishop Asbury and often filled appointments for him. George Leile and Andrew Bryan were preachers whose life history is of intense interest. "George Leile or Lisle, sometimes called George Sharp, was born in Virginia about 1750. His master (Mr. Sharp) some time before the American war removed and settled in Burke County, Georgia. Mr. Sharp was a Baptist and a deacon in a Baptist church, of which Rev. Matthew Moore was pastor. George was converted and baptized under Mr. Moore's ministry. The church gave him liberty to preach.

" About nine months after George Leile left Georgia, Andrew, surnamed Bryan, a man of good sense, great zeal, and some natural elocution, began to exhort his black brethren and friends. He and his followers were reprimanded and forbidden to engage further in religious exercises. He would, however, pray, sing, and encourage his fellow worshipers to seek the Lord.

" Their persecution was carried to an inhuman extent. Their evening assemblies were broken up and those found present were punished with stripes. Andrew Bryan and Sampson, his brother, converted about a year after him, were twice imprisoned, and they with about fifty others were whipped. When publicly whipped, and bleeding under his wounds, Andrew declared that he not only rejoiced to be whipped, but would gladly suffer death for the cause of Jesus Christ, and that while he had life and opportunity he would continue to preach Christ. He was faithful to his vow and, by patient continuance in well-doing, he put to silence and shamed his adversaries, and influential advocates and patrons were raised up for him. Liberty was given Andrew by the civil authority to continue his religious meetings under certain regulations. His master gave him the use of his barn at Brampton, three miles from Savannah, where he preached for two years with little interruption."

Lott Carey a free Virginia Negro " was evidently a man of superior intellect and force of character, as is evidenced from the fact that his reading took a wide range— from political economy, in Adam Smith's Wealth of Nations,' to the voyage of Captain Cook. That he was a worker as well as a preacher is true, for when he decided to go to Africa his employers offered to raise his salary from $800 to $1,000 a year. Remember that this was over eighty years ago. Carey was not seduced by such a flattering offer, for he was determined.

" His last sermon in the old First Church in Richmond must have been exceedingly powerful, for it was compared by an eye-witness, a resident of another state, to the burning, eloquent appeals of George Whitfield. Fancy him as he stands there in that historic building ringing the changes on the word ' freely,' depicting the willingness with which he was ready to give up his life for service in Africa.

" He, as you may already know, was the leader of the pioneer colony to Liberia, where he arrived even before the agent of the Colonization Society. In his new home his abilities were recognized, for he was made vice governor, and became governor in fact while Governor Ashmun was absent from the colony in this country. Carey did not allow his position to betray the cause of his people, for he did not hesitate to expose the duplicity of the Colonization Society and even to defy their authority, it would seem, in the interests of the people.

"While casting cartridges to defend the colonists against the natives in 1828, the accidental upsetting of a candle caused an explosion that resulted in his death.

"Carey is described as a typical Negro, six feet in height, of massive and erect frame, with the sinews of a Titan. He had a square face, keen eyes, and a grave countenance. His movements were measured; in short, he had all the bearing and dignity of a prince of the blood."

John Chavis was a full-blooded Negro, born in Granville County, N. C., near Oxford, in 1763. He was born free and was sent to Princeton, studying privately under Dr. Witherspoon, where he did well. He went to Virginia to preach to Negroes. In 1802, in the county court, his freedom and character were certified to and it was declared that he had passed " through a regular course of academic studies " at what is now Washington and Lee University. In 1805 he returned to North Carolina, where in 1809 he was made a licentiate in the Presbyterian Church and allowed to preach. His English was remarkably pure, his manner impressive, his explanations clear and concise.

For a long time he taught school and had the best whites as pupils—a United States senator, the sons of a chief justice of North Carolina, a governor of the state and many others. Some of his pupils boarded in the family, and his school was regarded as the best in the State. " All accounts agree that John Chavis was a gentleman," and he was received socially among the best whites and asked to table. In 1830 he was stopped from preaching by the law. Afterward he taught a school for free Negroes in Raleigh.

Henry Evans was a full-blooded Virginia free Negro, and was the pioneer of Methodism in Fayetteville, N. C. He found the Negroes there, about 1800, without any religious instruction. He began preaching and the town council ordered him away; he continued and whites came to hear him. Finally the white auditors outnumbered the blacks and sheds were erected for Negroes at the side of the church. The gathering became a regular Methodist Church, with a white and Negro membership, but Evans continued to preach. He exhibited " rare self-control before the most wretched of castes! Henry Evans did much good, but he would have done more good had his spirit been untrammeled by this sense of inferiority."

His dying words uttered as he stood, aged and bent beside his pulpit, are of singular pathos : " I have come to say my last word

to you. It is this: None but Christ.
Three times have I had my life in jeopardy
for preaching the gospel to you. Three
times I have broken ice on the edge of the
water and swam across the Cape Fear to
preach the gospel to you ; and, if in my last
hour I could trust to that, or anything but
Christ crucified, for my salvation, all should
be lost and my soul perish forever."

Early in the nineteenth century Ralph
Freeman was a slave in Anson County, N. C.
He was a full-blooded Negro, and was or-
dained and became an able Baptist preacher.
He baptized and administered communion,
and was greatly respected. When the
Baptists split on the question of missions he
sided with the anti-mission side. Finally
the law forbade him to preach.

Lunsford Lane was a Negro who bought
his freedom in Raleigh, N. C., by the
manufacture of smoking tobacco. He later
became a minister of the gospel, and had
the confidence of many of the best people.

The story of Jack of Virginia is best told in the words of a Southern writer :

" Probably the most interesting case in the whole South is that of an African preacher of Nottoway County, popularly known as 'Uncle Jack,' whose services to white and black were so valuable that a distinguished minister of the Southern Presbyterian Church felt called upon to memorialize his work in a biography.

" Kidnapped from his idolatrous parents in Africa, he was brought over in one of the last cargoes of slaves admitted to Virginia and sold to a remote and obscure planter in Nottoway County, a region at that time in the backwoods and destitute particularly as to religious life and instruction. He was converted under the occasional preaching of Rev. Dr. John Blair Smith, president of Hampden-Sidney College, and of Dr. William Hill and Dr. Archibald Alexander of Princeton, then young theologues, and by hearing the Scriptures read.

" Taught by his master's children to read, he became so full of the spirit and knowledge of the Bible that he was recognized among the whites as a powerful expounder of Christian doctrine, was licensed to preach by the Baptist Church, and preached from plantation to plantation within a radius of thirty miles, as he was invited by overseers or masters.   His freedom was purchased by a subscription of whites, and he was given a home and tract of land for his support. He organized a large and orderly Negro church, and exercised such a wonderful controlling influence over the private morals of his flock that masters, instead of punishing their slaves, often referred them to the discipline of their pastor, which they dreaded far more.

" He stopped a heresy among the Negroes of Southern Virginia, defeating in open argument a famous fanatical Negro preacher named Campbell, who advocated noise and ' the spirit ' against the Bible, and winning over Campbell's adherents in a body. For over forty years, and until he was nearly a hundred years of age, he labored successfully in public and private among black and whites, voluntarily giving up his preaching in obedience to the law of 1832, the result of 'Old Nat's war.'

"The most refined and aristocratic people paid tribute to him, and he was instrumental in the conversion of many whites. Says his biographer, Rev. Dr. William S. White: 'He was invited into their houses, sat with their families, took part in their social worship, sometimes leading the prayer at the family altar. Many of the most intelligent people attended upon his ministry and listened to his sermons with great delight. Indeed, previous to the year 1825, he was considered by the best judges to be the best preacher in that county. His opinions were respected, his advice followed, and yet he never betrayed the least symptoms of arrogance or self-conceit.

" ' His dwelling was a rude log cabin, his apparel of the plainest and coarsest materials.' This was because he wanted to be fully identified with his class. He refused gifts of better clothing, saying ' These clothes are a great deal better than are generally worn by people of my color, and besides if I wear finer ones I find I shall be obliged to think about them even at meeting.' "

Thus slowly, surely, the slave, in the persons of such exceptional men, appearing here and there at rare intervals, was persistently stretching upward. The Negroes bade fair in time to have their leaders. The new democratic evangelism began to encourage this, and then came the difficulty— the inevitable ethical paradox.

The good men of the South recognized the needs of the slaves. Here and there Negro ministers were arising. What now should be the policy ? On the part of the best thinkers it seemed as if men might strive here, in spite of slavery, after broth-

erhood ; that the slaves should be proselyted, taught religion, admitted to the
churches, and, notwithstanding their civil
station, looked upon as the spiritual
brothers of the white communicants. Much
was done to make this true. The conditions improved in a great many respects,
but no sooner was there a systematic effort
to teach the slaves, even though that teaching was confined to elementary religion,
than the various things followed that must
follow all intellectual awakenings.

We have had the same thing in our day.
A few Negroes of the South have been
taught, they consequently have begun to
think, they have begun to assert themselves, and suddenly men are face to face
with the fact that either one of two things
must happen—either they must stop teaching or these people are going to be men, not
serfs or slaves. Not only that, but to seek
to put an awakening people back to sleep
means revolt. It meant revolt in the

eighteenth century, when a series of insur-
rections and disturbances frightened the
South tremendously, not so much by their
actual extent as by the possibilities they
suggested. It was noticeable that many of
these revolts were led by preachers.

The revolution in Hayti greatly stirred
the South and induced South Carolina to
declare in 1800 :

" It shall not be lawful for any number
of slaves, free Negroes, mulattoes, or mesti-
zoes, even in company with white persons,
to meet together and assemble for the purpose of mental instruction or religious worship either before the rising of the sun or
after the going down of the same. And all
magistrates, sheriffs, militia officers, etc.,
etc., are hereby vested with power, etc., for
dispersing such assemblies."

On petition of the white churches the
rigor of this law was slightly abated in
1803 by a modification which forbade any
person, before nine o'clock in the evening,

" to break into a place of meeting wherein shall be assembled the members of any religious society in this State, provided a majority of them shall be white persons, or otherwise to disturb their devotions unless such persons, etc., so entering said place (of worship) shall first have obtained from some magistrate, etc., a warrant, etc., in case a magistrate shall be then actually within a distance of three miles from such place of meeting; otherwise the provisions, etc. (of the Act of 1800) to remain in full force."

So, too, in Virginia the Haytian revolt and the attempted insurrection under Gabriel in 1800 led to the Act of 1804, which forbade all evening meetings of slaves. This was modified in 1805 so as to allow a slave, in company with a white person, to listen to a white minister in the evening. A master was " allowed " to employ a religious teacher for his slaves. Mississippi passed similar restrictions.

By 1822 the rigor of the South Carolina laws in regard to Negro meetings had abated, especially in a city like Charleston, and one of the results was the Vesey plot.

" The sundry religious classes or congregations, with Negro leaders or local preachers, into which were formed the Negro members of the various churches of Charleston, furnished Vesey with the first rudiments of an organization, and at the same time with a singularly safe medium for conducting his underground agitation. It was customary, at that time, for these Negro congregations to meet for purposes of worship entirely free from the presence of whites.   Such meetings were afterward forbidden to be held except in the presence of at least one representative of the dominant race, but during the three or four years prior to the year 1822 they certainly offered Denmark Vesey regular, easy, and safe opportunity for preaching his gospel of liberty and hate.   And we are left in no doubt whatever in regard to the uses to which he put those gatherings of blacks.

" Like many of his race, he possessed the gift of gab, as the silver in the tongue and the gold in the full or thick-lipped mouth are oftentimes contemptuously characterized. And, like many of his race, he was a devoted student of the Bible, to whose interpretation he brought, like many other Bible students not confined to the Negro race, a good deal of imagination and not a little of superstition, which, with some natures, is perhaps but another name for the desires of the heart.

"Thus equipped, it is no wonder that Vesey, as he pored over the Old Testament scriptures, found many points of similitude in the history of the Jews and that of the slaves in the United States. They were both peculiar peoples. They were both Jehovah's peculiar peoples, one in the past, the other in the present. And it seemed to him that as Jehovah bent His ear, and bared

His arm once in behalf of the one, so would He do the same for the other. It was all vividly real to his thought, I believe, for to his mind thus had said the Lord.

" He ransacked the Bible for apposite and terrible texts whose commands in the olden times, to the olden people, were no less imperative upon the new times and the new people. This new people were also commanded to arise and destroy their enemies and the city in which they dwelt, ' both man and woman, young and old, with the edge of the sword.' Believing superstitiously as he did in the stern and Nemesis-like God of the Old Testament he looked confidently for a day of vengeance and retribution for the blacks. He felt, I doubt not, something peculiarly applicable to his enterprise and intensely personal to himself in the stern and exultant prophecy of Zachariah, fierce and sanguinary words, which were constantly in his mouth : ' Then shall the Lord go forth and fight against those nations as when He fought in the day of battle.' According to Vesey's lurid exegesis 'those nations' in the text meant beyond peradventure the cruel masters, and Jehovah was to go forth to fight them for the poor slaves and on whichever side fought that day the Almighty God on that side would assuredly rest victory and deliverance.

"It will not be denied that Vesey's plan contemplated the total annihilation of the white population of Charleston. Nursing for many dark years the bitter wrongs of himself and race had filled him without doubt with a mad spirit of revenge and had given to him a decided predilection for shedding the blood of his oppressors. But if he intended to kill them to satisfy a desire for vengeance he intended to do so also on broader ground. The conspirators, he argued, had no choice in the matter, but were compelled to adopt a policy of extermination by the necessity of their position.

The liberty of the blacks was in the balance of fate against the lives of the whites. He could strike that balance in favor of the blacks only by the total destruction cf the whites. Therefore the whites, men, women, and children, were doomed to death." [1]

Vesey's plot was well laid, but the conspirators were betrayed.

Less than ten years after this plot was discovered and Vesey and his associates hanged, there broke out the Nat Turner insurrection in Virginia. Turner was himself a preacher.

"He was a Christian and a man. He was conscious that he was a Man and not a ' thing '; therefore, driven by religious fanaticism, he undertook a difficult and bloody task. Nathaniel Turner was born in Southampton County, Virginia, October 2, 1800. His master was one Benjamin Turner, a very wealthy and aristocratic man. He owned many slaves, and was a cruel and

[1] Grimke : " Right on the Scaffold."

exacting master. Young 'Nat' was born of slave parents, and carried to his grave many of the superstitions and traits of his father and mother. The former was a preacher, the latter a 'mother in Israel.' Both were unlettered but, nevertheless, very pious people.

"The mother began when Nat was quite young to teach him that he was born, like Moses, to be the deliverer of his race. She would sing to him snatches of wild, rapturous songs and repeat portions of prophecy she had learned from the preachers of those times. Nat listened with reverence and awe, and believed everything his mother said. He imbibed the deep religious character of his parents, and soon manifested a desire to preach. He was solemnly set apart to 'the gospel ministry' by his father, the church, and visiting preachers. He was quite low in stature, dark, and had the genuine African features. His eyes were small but sharp, and gleamed like fire when

he was talking about his 'mission' or
preaching from some prophetic passage of
scripture.    It is said that he never laughed.
He was a dreamy sort of a man, and avoided
the crowd.

" Like Moses he lived in the solitudes of
the mountains and brooded over the condition of his people.    There was something
grand to him in the rugged scenery that
nature had surrounded him with.    He believed that he was a prophet, a leader raised
up by God to burst the bolts of the prison-
house and set the oppressed free.    The thun-
der, the hail, the storm-cloud, the air, the
earth, the stars, at which he would sit and
gaze half the night all spake the language of
the God of the oppressed.    He was seldom
seen in a large company, and never drank a
drop of ardent spirits.    Like John the Baptist, when he had delivered his message, he
would  retire to the fastness of the mountain
or seek the desert, where he could meditate
upon his great work."

In the impression of the Richmond *Enquirer* of the 30th of August, 1831, the first editorial or leader is under the caption of " The Banditte." The editor says :

" They remind one of a parcel of blood-thirsty wolves rushing down from the Alps ; or, rather, like a former incursion of the Indians upon the white settlements. Nothing is spared ; neither age nor sex respected —the helplessness of women and children pleads in vain for mercy. . . . The case of Nat Turner warns us. No black man ought to be permitted to turn preacher through the country. The law must be enforced, or the tragedy of Southampton appeals to us in vain."

Mr. Gray, the man to whom Turner made his confession before dying, said :

" It has been said that he was ignorant and cowardly and that his object was to murder and rob for the purpose of obtaining money to make his escape. It is notorious that he was never known to have a dollar in his life, to swear an oath, or drink a drop of spirits. As to his ignorance, he certainly never had the advantages of an education, but he can read and write, and for natural intelligence and quickness of apprehension is surpassed by few men I have ever seen. As to his being a coward, his reason as given for not resisting Mr. Phipps, shows the decision of his character. When he saw Mr. Phipps present his gun, he said he knew it was impossible for him to escape as the woods were full of men. He, therefore, thought it was better for him to surrender and trust to fortune for his escape.

" He is a complete fanatic or plays his part most admirably. On other subjects he possesses an uncommon share of intelligence, with a mind capable of attaining anything, but warped and perverted by the influence of early impressions. He is below the ordinary stature, though strong and active, having the true Negro face, every feature of which is strongly marked.

" I shall not attempt to describe the effect of his narrative, as told and commented on by himself, in the condemned hole of the prison; the calm deliberate composure with which he spoke of his late deeds and intentions; the expression of his fiend-like face when excited by enthusiasm, still bearing the stains of the blood of the helpless innocence about him, clothed with rags and covered with chains, yet daring to raise his manacled hand to Heaven, with a spirit soaring above the attributes of man. I looked on him and the blood curdled in my veins." [1]

The Turner insurrection is so connected with the economic revolution which enthroned cotton that it marks an epoch in the history of the slave. A wave of legislation passed over the South prohibiting the slaves from learning to read and write, forbidding Negroes to preach, and interfering with Negro religious meetings.

[1] "The Negro Church," Atlanta University Publications, No. 8.

Virginia declared, in 1831, that neither slaves nor free Negroes might preach, nor could they attend religious service at night without permission. In North Carolina slaves and free Negroes were forbidden to preach, exhort or teach " in any prayer-meeting or other association for worship where slaves of different families are collected together" on penalty of not more than thirty-nine lashes. Maryland and Georgia had similar laws. The Mississippi law of 1831 said : It is "unlawful for any slave, free Negro, or mulatto to preach the gospel" upon pain of receiving thirty-nine lashes upon the naked back of the presumptuous preacher. If a Negro received written permission from his master he might preach to the Negroes in his immediate neighborhood, providing six respectable white men, owners of slaves, were present. In Alabama the law of 1832 prohibited the assembling of more than five male slaves at any place off the plantation to which they belonged, but nothing in the act was to be considered as forbidding attendance at places of public worship held by white persons. No slave or free person of color was permitted to "preach, exhort, or harangue any slave or slaves, or free persons of color, except in the presence of five respectable slaveholders, or unless the person preaching was licensed by some regular body of professing Christians in the neighborhood, to whose society or church the Negroes addressed properly belonged."

In the District of Columbia the free Negroes began to leave white churches in 1831 and to assemble in their own.

Thus it was that through the fear of insurrection, the economic press of the new slavery that was arising, and the new significance of slavery in the economics of the South, the strife for spiritual brotherhood was given up. Slavery became distinctly a matter of race and not of status. Long years before, the white servants had been freed and only black servants were left ; now social condition came to be not simply a matter of slavery but a matter of belonging to the black race, so that even the free Negroes began to be disfranchised and put into the caste system (see Note 23).

A new adjustment of ethics and religion had to be made to meet this new situation, and in the adjustment, no matter what might be said or thought, the Negro and slavery had to be the central thing.

In the adjustment of religion and ethics that was made for the new slavery, under the cotton kingdom, there was in the first place a distinct denial of human brotherhood. These black men were not men in the sense that white men were men. They were different—different in kind, different in origin ; they had different diseases (see Note 24) ; they had different feelings ; they were not to be treated the same ; they were not looked upon as the same ; they were altogether apart and, while perhaps

they had certain low sensibilities and
aspirations, yet so far as this world is concerned, there could be with them neither
human nor spiritual brotherhood.

The only status that they could possibly
occupy was the status of slaves. They could
not get along as freemen ; they could not
work as freemen ; it was utterly unthinkable that people should live with them free.
This was the philosophy that was worked
out gradually, with exceptions here and
there, and that was thought through,
written on, preached from the pulpits and
taught in the homes, until people in the
South believed it as they believed the rising
and the setting of the sun.

As this became more and more the ortho-
dox ethical opinion, heretics appeared in the
land as they always do. But intolerance and
anathema met them. In community after
community there was a demand for orthodoxy on this one burning question of the
economic and religious South, and the

heretics were driven out. The Quakers left North Carolina, the abolitionists either left Virginia or ceased to talk, and throughout the South those people who dared to think otherwise were left silent or dead (see Note 25).

So long as slavery was an economic success this orthodoxy was all powerful; when signs of economic distress appeared it became intolerant and aggressive. A great moral battle was impending in the South, but political turmoil and a development of northern thought so rapid as to be unintelligible in the South stopped this development forcibly. War came and the hatred and moral bluntness incident to war, and men crystallized in their old thought.

The matter now could no longer be argued and thought out, it became a matter of tradition, of faith, of family and personal honor. There grew up therefore after the war a new predicament; a new-old paradox. Upon the whites hung the curse of the past ; because they had not settled their labor problem then, they must settle the problem now in the face of upheaval and handicapped by the natural advance of the world.

So after the war and even to this day, the religious and ethical life of the South bows beneath this burden. Shrinking from facing the burning ethical questions that front it unrelentingly, the Southern Church clings all the more closely to the letter of a worn out orthodoxy, while its inner truer soul crouches before and fears to answer the problem of eight million black neighbors. It therefore assiduously " preaches Christ crucified," in prayer meeting *patois*, and crucifies " Niggers " in unrelenting daily life.

While the Church in the North, all too slowly but surely is struggling up from the ashes of a childish faith in myth and miracle, and beginning to preach a living gospel of civic virtue, peace and good will and a crusade against lying, stealing and snobbery, the Southern church for the most part is still murmuring of modes of " baptism," " infant damnation " and the " divine plan of creation."

Thus the post-bellum ethical paradox of the South is far more puzzling than the economic paradox. To be sure there is leaven in the lump. There are brave voices here and there, but they are easily drowned by social tyranny in the South and by indifference and sensationalism in the North (see Note 26).

First of all the result of the war was the complete expulsion of Negroes from white churches. Little has been said of this, but perhaps it was in itself the most singular and tremendous result of slavery. The Methodist Church South simply set its Negro members bodily out of doors. They did it with some consideration for their feelings, with as much kindliness as crass unkindliness can show, but they virtually said to all their black members—to the black mammies whom they have almost fulsomely praised and whom they remember in such astonishing numbers to-day, to the polite and deferential old servant, to whose character they build monuments—they said to them : " You cannot worship God with us." There grew up, therefore, the Colored Methodist Episcopal Church.

Flagrantly unchristian as this course was, it was still in some ways better than the absolute withdrawal of church fellowship on the part of the Baptists, or the policy of Episcopalians, which was simply that of studied neglect and discouragement which froze, harried, and well nigh invited the black communicants to withdraw.

From the North now came those Negro church bodies born of color discrimination in Philadelphia and New York in the eighteenth century, and thus a Christianity absolutely divided along the color line arose. There may be in the South a black

man belonging to a white church to-day but
if so, he must be very old and very feeble.
This anomaly—this utter denial of the very
first principles of the ethics of Jesus Christ
—is to-day so deep seated and unquestion-
able a principle of Southern Christianity
that its essential heathenism is scarcely
thought of, and every revival of religion in
this section banks its spiritual riches solidly
and unmovedly against the color line,
without conscious question.

Among the Negroes the results are equally
unhappy. They needed ethical leadership,
spiritual guidance, and religious instruction.
If the Negroes of the South are to any degree immoral, sexually unchaste, crimi-
nally inclined, and religiously ignorant,
what right has the Christian South even to
whisper reproach or accusation? How often have they raised a finger to assume
spiritual or religious guardianship over
those victims of their past system of economic and social life?

Left thus unguided the Negroes, with some help from such Northern white churches as dared, began their own religious upbuilding (see Note 27). They faced tremendous difficulties—lack of ministers, money, and experience. Their churches could not be simply centres of religious life —because in the poverty of their organized efforts all united striving tended to centre in this one social organ. The Negro Church consequently became a great social institution with some ethical ideas but with those ethical ideas warped and changed and perverted by the whole history of the past; with memories, traditions, and rites of heathen worship, of intense emotionalism, trance, and weird singing.

And above all, there brooded over and in the church the sense of all their grievances. Whatsoever their own shortcomings might be, at least they knew that they were not guilty of hypocrisy; they did not cry " Whosoever will " and then brazenly ostracize half the world. They knew that they opened their doors and hearts wide to all people that really wanted to come in and they looked upon the white churches not as examples but with a sort of silent contempt and a real inner questioning of the genuineness of their Christianity.

On the other hand, so far as the white post-bellum Christian church is concerned, I can conceive no more pitiable paradox than that of the young white Christian in the South to-day who really believes in the ethics of Jesus Christ. What can he think when he hangs upon his church doors the sign that I have often seen, " All are welcome." He knows that half the population of his city would not dare to go inside that church. Or if there was any fellowship between Christians, white and black, it would be after the manner explained by a white Mississippi clergyman in all seriousness : " The whites and Negroes understand each other here perfectly, sir, perfectly ; if they come to my church they take a seat in the gallery. If I go to theirs, they invite me to the front pew or the platform."

Once in Atlanta a great revival was going on in a prominent white church. The people were at fever heat, the minister was preaching and calling " Come to Jesus." Up the aisle tottered an old black man—he was an outcast, he had wandered in there aimlessly off the streets, dimly he had comprehended this call and he came tottering and swaying up the aisle. What was the result? It broke up the revival. There was no disturbance ; he was gently led out, but that sudden appearance of a black face spoiled the whole spirit of the thing and the revival was at an end.

Who can doubt that if Christ came to Georgia to-day one of His first deeds would be to sit down and take supper with black men, and who can doubt the outcome if He did ?

It is this tremendous paradox of a Christianity that theoretically opens the church to all men and yet closes it forcibly and insultingly in the face of black men and that does this not simply in the visible church but even more harshly in the spiritual fellowship of human souls—it is this that makes the ethical and religious problem in the South to-day of such tremendous importance, and that gives rise to the one thing which it seems to me is the most difficult in the Southern situation and that is, the tendency to deny the truth, the tendency to lie when the real situation comes up because the truth is too hard to face. This lying about the situation of the South has not been simply a political subterfuge against the dangers of ignorance, but is a sort of gasping inner revolt against acknowledging the real truth of the ethical conviction which every true Southerner must feel, namely: that the South is eternally and fundamentally wrong on the plain straight question of the equality of souls before God—of the inalienable rights of all men.

Here are men—they are aspiring, they are struggling piteously forward, they have frequent instances of ability, there is no doubt as to the tremendous strides which certain classes of Negroes have made—how shall they be treated? That they should be treated as men, of course, the best class of Southerners know and sometimes acknowledge. And yet they believe, and believe with fierce conviction, that it is impossible to treat Negroes as men, and still live with them. Right there is the paradox which they face daily and which is daily stamping hypocrisy upon their religion and upon their land.

Their irresistible impulse in this awful dilemma is to point to and emphasize the Negro's degradation, even though they know that it is not the degraded Negro whom they most fear, ostracize, and fight to keep down, but rather the rising, ambitious Negro.

If my own city of Atlanta had offered it to-day the choice between 500 Negro college graduates—forceful, busy, ambitious men of property and self-respect, and 500 black cringing vagrants and criminals, the popular vote in favor of the criminals would be simply overwhelming. Why? because they want Negro crime? No, not that they fear Negro crime less, but that they fear Negro ambition and success more. They can deal with crime by chain-gang and lynch law, or at least they think they can, but the South can conceive neither machinery nor place for the educated, self-reliant, self-assertive black man.

Are a people pushed to such moral extremities, the ones whose level-headed, unbiased statements of fact concerning the Negro can be relied upon? Do they really know the Negro? Can the nation expect

of them the poise and patience necessary
for the settling of a great social problem?

Not only is there then this initial false-
ness when the South excuses its ethical
paradox by pointing to the low condition of
the Negro masses, but there is also a strange
blindness in failing to see that every pound
of evidence to prove the present degradation of black men but adds to the crushing
weight of indictment against their past
treatment of this race.

A race is not made in a single generation.
If they accuse Negro women of lewdness
and Negro men of monstrous crime, what
are they doing but advertising to the world
the shameless lewdness of those Southern
men who brought millions of mulattoes
into the world, and whose deeds throughout the South and particularly in Virginia,
the mother of slavery, have left but few
prominent families whose blood does not
to-day course in black veins? Suppose to-

day Negroes do steal; who was it that for centuries made stealing a virtue by stealing their labor? Have not laziness and listlessness always been the followers of slavery? If these ten millions are ignorant by whose past law and mandate and present practice is this true?

The truth then cannot be controverted. The present condition of the Negro in America is better than the history of slavery proves we might reasonably expect. With the help of his friends, North and South, and despite the bitter opposition of his foes, South and North, he has bought twelve million acres of land, swept away two-thirds of his illiteracy, organized his church, and found leadership and articulate voice. Yet despite this the South, Christian and unchristian, with only here and there an exception, still stands like a rock wall and says: Negroes are not men and must not be treated as men.

When now the world faces such an absolute ethical contradiction, the truth is nearer than it seems.

It stands to-day perfectly clear and plain despite all sophistication and false assumption : If the contention of the South is true—that Negroes cannot by reason of hereditary inferiority take their places in modern civilization beside white men, then the South owes it to the world and to its better self to give the Negro every chance to prove this. To make the assertion dogmatically and then resort to all means which retard and restrict Negro development is not simply to stand convicted of insincerity before the civilized world, but, far worse than that, it is to make a nation of naturally generous, honest people to sit humiliated before their own consciences.

I believe that a straightforward, honorable treatment of black men according to their desert and achievement, will soon settle the Negro problem. If the South is right few will rise to a plane that will make their social reception a matter worth consideration; few will gain the sobriety and industry which will deserve the ballot; and few will achieve such solid moral character as will give them welcome to the fellowship of the church. If, on the other hand, Negroes with the door of opportunity thrown wide do become men of industry and achievement, of moral strength and even genius, then such rise will silence the South with an eternal silence.

The nation that enslaved the Negro owes him this trial; the section that doggedly and unreasonably kept him in slavery owes him at least this chance; and the church which professes to follow Jesus Christ and does not insist on this elemental act of justice merits the denial of the Master— "*I never knew you.*"

This, then, is the history of those mighty moral battles in the South which have given us the Negro problem. And the last great battle is not a battle of South or East, of black or white, but of all of us. The path to racial peace is straight but narrow —its following to-day means tremendous fight against inertia, prejudice, and intrenched snobbery. But it is the duty of men, it is a duty of the church, to face the problem. Not only is it their duty to face it—they *must* face it, it is impossible not to, the very attempt to ignore it is assuming an attitude. It is a problem not simply of political expediency, of economic success, but a problem above all of religious and social life; and it carries with it not simply a demand for its own solution, but beneath it lies the whole question of the real intent of our civilization : Is the civilization of the United States Christian ?

It is a matter of grave consideration what answer we ought to give to that question. The precepts of Jesus Christ cannot but mean that Christianity consists of an attitude of humility, of a desire for peace, of a disposition to treat our brothers as we would have our brothers treat us, of mercy and charity toward our fellow men, of willingness to suffer persecution for right ideals and in general of love not only toward our friends but even toward our enemies.

Judged by this, it is absurd to call the practical religion of this nation Christian. We are not humble, we are impudently proud; we are not merciful, we are unmerciful toward friend and foe; we are not peaceful nor peacefully inclined as our armies and battle-ships declare; we do not want to be martyrs, we would much rather be thieves and liars so long as we can be rich; we do not seek continuously, and prayerfully inculcate, love and justice for our fellow men, but on the contrary the treatment of the poor, the unfortunate, and the black within our borders is almost a national crime.

The problem that lies before Christians is tremendous (see Note 28), and the answer must begin not by a slurring over of the

one problem where these different tests of
Christianity are most flagrantly disre-
garded, but it must begin by a girding of
ourselves and a determination to see that
justice is done in this country to the
humblest and blackest as well as to the
greatest and whitest of our citizens.

Now a word especially about the Episcopal church, whose position toward its
Negro communicants is peculiar. I appreciate this position and speak of it specifically because I am one of those communicants. For four generations my family
has belonged to this church and I belong to
it, not by personal choice, not because I feel
myself welcome within its portals, but
simply because I refuse to be read outside
of a church which is mine by inheritance
and the service of my fathers. When the
Episcopal church comes, as it does come to-
day, to the Parting of the Ways, to the
question as to whether its record in the
future is going to be, on the Negro problem,

as disgraceful as it has been in the past, I
feel like appealing to all who are members
of that church to remember that after all
it is a church of Jesus Christ.    Your creed
and your duty enjoin upon you one, and
only one, course of procedure.

In the real Christian church there is
neither black nor white, rich nor poor, bar-
barian, Scythian, bond nor free, but all
stand equal before the face of the Master.
If you find that you cannot treat your Negro members as fellow Christians then do
not deceive yourselves into thinking that
the differences that you make or are going
to make in their treatment are made for
their good or for the service of the world ;
do not entice them to ask for a separation
which your unchristian conduct forces them
to prefer ; do not pretend that the distinctions which you make toward them are distinctions which are made for the larger good
of men, but simply confess in humility and
self-abasement that you are not able to live

up to your Christian vows; that you cannot treat these men as brothers and therefore you are going to set them aside and let them go their half-tended way.

I should be sorry, I should be grieved more than I can say, to see that which happened in the Southern Methodist Church and that which is practically happening in the Presbyterian Church, and that which will come in other sects—namely, a segregation of Negro Christians, come to be true among Episcopalians. It would be a sign of Christian disunity far more distressing than sectarianism. I should therefore deplore it; and yet I am also free to say that unless this church is prepared to treat its Negro members with exactly the same consideration that other members receive, with the same brotherhood and fellowship, the same encouragement to aspiration, the same privileges, similarly trained priests and similar preferment for them, then I should a great deal rather see them set aside than to see a continuation of present injustice.  All I ask is that when you do this you do it with an open and honest statement of the real reasons and not with statements veiled by any hypocritical excuses.

I am therefore above all desirous that the younger men and women who are to-day taking up the leadership of this great group of men, who wish the world better and work toward that end, should begin to see the real significance of this step and of the great problem behind it.  It is not a problem simply of the South, not a problem simply of this country, it is a problem of the world.

As I have said elsewhere: "Most men are colored.  A belief in humanity is above all a belief in colored men."  If you cannot get on with colored men in America you cannot get on with the modern world ; and if you cannot work with the humanity of this world how shall your souls ever tune with the myriad sided souls of worlds to come ?

It may be that the price of the black man's survival in America and in the modern world, will be a long and shameful night of subjection to caste and segregation. If so, he will pay it, doggedly, silently, un-falteringly, for the sake of human liberty and the souls of his children's children. But as he stoops he will remember the in-dignation of that Jesus who cried, yonder behind heaving seas and years : " Woe unto you scribes and Pharisees, hypocrites, that strain out a gnat and swallow a camel,"— as if God cared a whit whether His Sons are born of maid, wife or widow so long as His church sits deaf to His own calling :

" Ho ! every one that thirsteth, come ye to the waters and he that hath no money ; come ye, buy and eat ; yea, come, buy wine and milk without money and without price ! "

# NOTES

## TO CHAPTERS III AND IV

## Note 1

"The history of slavery and the slave trade after 1820 must be read in the light of the industrial revolution through which the civilized world passed in the first half of the nineteenth century. Between the years 1775 and 1825 occurred economic events and changes of the highest importance and widest influence. Though all branches of the industry felt the impulse of this new industrial life, yet, if we consider single industries, cotton manufacture has, during the nineteenth century, made the most magnificent and gigantic advances."

This fact is easily explained by the remarkable series of inventions that revolutionized this industry between 1738 and 1830, including Arkwright's, Watt's, Compton's, and Cartwright's epoch making contrivances.   The effect which these inventions had on the manufacture of cotton goods is best illustrated by the fact that in England, the chief cotton market of the world, the consumption of raw cotton rose steadily from 13,000 bales in 1781, to 572,000 in 1820, to 871,000 in 1830, and to 3,366,000 in 1860.   Very early, therefore, came the query whence the supply of raw cotton was to come.   Tentative experiments on the rich, broad fields of the Southern United States, together with the indispensable invention of Whitney's cotton gin, soon answered this question.   A new economic future was opened up to this land, and immediately the whole South began to extend its cotton culture, and more and more to throw its whole energy into this one staple.

Here it was that the fatal mistake of compromising with slavery in the beginning, and of the policy of *laissez-faire* pursued thereafter, became painfully manifest; for, instead now of a healthy, normal, economic development along proper industrial lines, we have the abnormal and fatal rise of a slave-labor, large-farming system, which, before it was realized, had so intertwined itself with and braced itself upon the economic forces of an industrial age, that a vast and terrible civil war was necessary to displace it. The tendencies to a patriarchal serfdom, recognized in the age of Washington and Jefferson, began slowly but surely to disappear; and in the second quarter of the century Southern slavery was irresistibly changing from a family institution to an industrial system.

DuBois, "Suppression of the Slave Trade," p. 151.

A list of the chief inventions most graphically illustrates the above : —

1738, John Jay, fly shuttle.

John Wyatt, spinning by rollers.

1748, Lewis Paul, carding machine.

1760, Robert Kay, drop box.

1769, Richard Arkwright, water-frame and throstle.

James Watt, steam-engine.

1772, James Lees, improvements on carding-machine.

1775, Richard Arkwright, series of combinations.

1779, Samuel Compton, mule.

1785, Edmund Cartwright, power-loom.

1803–4, Radcliffe and Johnson, dressing-machine.

1817, Roberts, fly-frame.

1818, William Eaton, self-acting frame.

1825–30, Roberts, improvements on mule.

Cf. Baines, " History of the Cotton Manufactures," pp. 116–23 ; " Encyclopædia Britannica," 9th ed., article " Cotton."


NOTE 2

In 1832, Alabama declared that "any person or persons who shall attempt to teach any free person of color or slave to spell, read, or write, shall, upon conviction thereof by indictment, be fined in a sum not less than $250, nor more than $500."

Georgia, in 1770, fined any person who taught a slave to read or write twenty pounds. In 1829 the State enacted :

" If any slave, Negro or free person of color, or any white person, shall teach any other slave, Negro or free person of color to read or write, either written or printed characters, the same free person of color or slave shall be punished by fine and whipping, or fine or whipping, at the discretion of the court ; and if a white person so offend, he, she or they shall be punished with a fine not exceeding $500 and imprisonment in the common jail at the discretion of the court."

In 1833 this law was put into the penal code, with additional penalties for using slaves in printing offices to set type. These laws were violated sometimes by individual masters, and clandestine schools were opened for Negroes in some of the cities before the war. In 1850 and thereafter there was some agitation to repeal these laws and a bill to that effect failed in the Senate of Georgia by two or three votes.

Louisiana, in 1830, declared that "All persons who shall teach or permit or cause to be taught any slave to read or write shall be imprisoned not less than one month nor more than twelve months."

Missouri, in 1847, passed an act saying that "No person shall keep or teach any school for the instruction of Negroes or mulattoes in reading or writing in this state."

North Carolina had schools supported by free Negroes up until 1835, when they were abolished by law.

South Carolina, in 1740, declared : "Whereas, the having of slaves taught to write or suffering them to be employed in writing may be attended with inconveniences, be it enacted, that all and every person and persons whatsoever who shall here-

after teach or cause any slave or slaves to be
taught, or shall use or employ any slave as
a scribe in any manner of writing whatever,
hereafter taught to write, every such person
or persons shall for every such offense for-
feit the sum of £100 current money."

In 1800 and 1833 the teaching of free
Negroes was restricted : " And if any free
person of color or slave shall keep any
school or other places of instruction for
teaching any slave or free person of color to
read or write, such free person of color or
slave shall be liable to the same fine, im-
prisonment and corporal punishment as by
this act are imposed and inflicted on free
persons of color and slaves for teaching
slaves to write." Other sections prohibited
white persons from teaching slaves. Ap-
parently whites might teach free Negroes to
some extent.

Virginia, in 1819, forbade " all meetings
or assemblages of slaves or free Negroes or
mulattoes mixing and associating with such

slaves, . . . at any school or schools for teaching them reading and writing, either in the day or night." Nevertheless free Negroes kept schools for themselves until the Nat Turner Insurrection, when it was enacted, 1831, that "all meetings of free Negroes or mulattoes at any school-house, church, meeting-house or other place, for teaching them reading and writing, either in the day or night, under whatsoever pretext, shall be deemed and considered an unlawful assembly." This law was carefully enforced.

In the Northern States few actual prohibitory laws were enacted, but in Connecticut, New York, Pennsylvania, Ohio and elsewhere, mob violence frequently arose against Negro schools, and in Connecticut the teaching of Negroes was restricted as follows in 1833: "No person shall set up or establish in this state any school, academy or other literary institution for the instruction or education of colored persons who are not inhabitants of this State, or harbor or board, for the purpose of attending or being taught or instructed in any such school, academy or literary institution any colored person who is not an inhabitant of any town in this State, without the consent, in writing, first obtained, of a majority of the civil authority, and also of the selectmen of the town in which each school, academy or literary institution is situated." This was especially directed against the famous Prudence Crandall school, and was repeated in 1838.

Ohio decreed, in 1829, that " the attendance of black or mulatto persons be specifically prohibited, but all taxes assessed upon the property of colored persons for school purposes should be appropriated to their instruction and no other purpose." This prohibition was enforced, but the second clause was a dead letter for twenty years. Cf. Atlanta University Publications, No. 6.

NOTE 3

Cf. Cairnes' " Slave Power."


NOTE 4

Stephen A. Douglas said " that there was
not the shadow of doubt that the slave-
trade had been carried on quite extensively
for a long time back, and that there had
been more slaves imported into the Southern
States, during the last year, than had ever
been imported before in any one year, even
when the slave-trade was legal.  It was his
confident belief, that over fifteen thousand
slaves had been brought into this country
during the past year (1859).  He had seen,
with his own eyes, three hundred of those
recently-imported, miserable beings, in a
slave-pen in Vicksburg, Miss., and also
large numbers at Memphis, Tenn."  It was
currently reported that depots for these
slaves existed in over twenty large cities
and towns in the South, and an interested
person boasted to a senator, about 1860,

that " twelve vessels would discharge their living freight upon our shores within ninety days from the 1st of June last," and that between sixty and seventy cargoes had been successfully introduced in the last eighteen months. (Cf. DuBois : " Slave Trade," ch. xi.)

## Note 5

Cf. Olmsted's " Journeys " and Helper's " Impending Crisis."

## Note 6

Has not the time come for characterizing war plainly and ceasing to envelope it in a haze of sentimental lies? We have near worshiped the Civil War for a generation, when in truth it was a disgrace to civilization and we know it.

## Note 7

Cf. Blaine : " Twenty Years in Congress "; " American Political Science Review," Vol. 1, pp. 44–61 ; *e. g.*, " South Carolina, besides thus minutely regulating the labor of

Negroes under contract, prohibited them from practicing the 'art, trade or business of an artisan, mechanic, or shopkeeper,' or any other trade or business on their own account without paying an annual license fee to the district judge. And no Negro could obtain a license who had not served a term of 'apprenticeship' at the trade. Tennessee also required licenses; and Mississippi required Negroes to have written evidence of their home and employment. Mississippi also prohibited the renting or leasing of any land to Negroes, except in incorporated towns and cities." Louisiana had perhaps the most outrageous provisions.

### Note 8

Albion W. Tourgee said: "They instituted a public school system in a region where public schools had been unknown. They opened the ballot-box and the jury-box to thousands of white men who had been debarred from them by a lack of

earthly possessions. They introduced home
rule in the South. They abolished the
whipping-post, the branding-iron, the stocks
and other barbarous forms of punishment
which had up to that time prevailed. They
reduced capital felonies from about twenty
to two or three. In an age of extravagance
they were extravagant in the sums appropriated for public works. In all that time
no man's rights of person were invaded
under the forms of law." Thomas E. Miller,
a Negro member of the late Constitutional
Convention of South Carolina, said : " The
gentleman from Edgefield (Mr. Tillman)
speaks of the piling of the State debt ; of
jobbery and peculation during the period
between 1869 and 1873 in South Carolina,
but he has not found voice eloquent enough
nor pen exact enough to mention those im-
perishable gifts bestowed upon South Carolina between 1873 and 1876 by Negro leg-
islators—the laws relative to finance, the
building of penal and charitable institu-

tions, and, greatest of all, the establishment
of the public school system.  Starting as
infants in legislation in 1869, many wise
measures were not thought of, many in-
judicious acts were passed.  But in the
administration of affairs for the next four
years, having learned by experience the result of bad acts, we immediately passed
reformatory laws touching every depart-
ment of state, county, municipal and town
governments.  These enactments are to-day
upon the statute books of South Carolina.
They stand as living witnesses of the
Negro's fitness to vote and legislate upon
the rights of mankind."

Cf. Love's "Disfranchisement of the
Negro," p. 10.

### NOTE 9

Cf. "The Economic Future of the Negro," in papers and proceedings of the eighteenth Annual Meeting, American Economic Association, pp. 219–42.

## NOTE 10

See Alabama Laws on Labor Contracts.

## NOTE 11

See Laws of Alabama, 1906–1907.

## NOTE 12

See Laws of South Carolina, 1906–1907.

## NOTE 13

Cf. Bulletin Number 8, 12th United States Census.

## NOTE 14

This statement when made was challenged by a Virginia rector. Let John Sharp Williams, minority leader of the House of Representatives answer him.

" It is the physical presence of the Negro which constitutes the Negro problem and the race issue. It is not the fact that the Negro can vote in the South, because, as a matter of fact, he cannot and does not. The Negro problem would be just as troublesome as it is to-day if the fifteenth amendment were repealed.  The fifteenth amendment touches it only on its political or voting side, where the trouble is cured already in the South.  It is true that. the Negro does vote in Ohio, Illinois and New Jersey and various other places.  But the people of those states could to-morrow, if they wanted to, get rid of his vote, just as we have got rid of it in Mississippi.  The very fact that they have not done it is proof of the fact that they do not want to do it, and that very fact is the death-blow of the Vardaman agitation."

Negroes are disfranchised by legal and illegal methods and by unfair administration of the law.  The " white " primary is a wide-spread subterfuge : to the democratic primary election all white men are admitted without question, and no Negro under any circumstances.  The verdict of the primary is then registered in a farce " election."  In Atlanta, *e. g.*, at the " election " 700 votes

are cast in a city of 100,000! The success
of the " white " primary depends of course
(*a*) on the illegal power of the party chiefs
to exclude any votes they choose on any pretext and (*b*) on the absolute and unfair control of election machinery and returns by
one party and (*c*) on public acquiescence in
this travesty on popular government.

## NOTE 15

The Atlanta riot had two distinct phases :
first, Saturday, the killing of innocent and
surprised Negroes by a white mob; then a
lull when blacks rapidly armed themselves ;
finally the attempt to renew the assault by
a crowd mingled with county policemen,
who were repulsed by a fierce defense by
Negroes ; these Negroes were afterward ac-
quitted of murder by a southern jury. The
number of white and black killed in that
encounter will never be known, but it
stopped the riot. Cf. " World To-Day,"
Nov. 1906.

NOTE 16

The executive officials of the miners in Alabama consist of four whites and four Negroes.

NOTE 17

Ten good references on the economic history of the Negro and slavery are:

1. Kemble, Fanny, " A Journal of a Residence on a Georgia Plantation," N. Y., 1863.   337 pp. 12mo.

2.   Olmsted, F. L, " A Journey in the Sea Board Slave States," N. Y., 1856.   723 pp. 12mo.

3.   Cairnes, J. E., " The Slave Power : Its Character, Career, and Probable Designs," London, 1862.   304 pp, 2d ed. N. Y. 410 pp.

4.   United States 12th Census, Bulletin No. 8: " Negroes in United States," by W. F. Wilcox and W. E. B. DuBois, Wash., 1904, 333 pp.

5.   " The Philadelphia Negro " (Publica-

tions of the University of Pennsylvania)
520 pp. Ginn.

6. " The Suppression of the Slave Trade "
(Harvard Historical Monographs, No. 1)
335 pp. Longmans, 1896.

7. Atlanta University Publications :
   No. 3, " Efforts for Social Betterment,"
   66 pp. 1898.
   No. 4, " The Negro in Business," 77 pp.
   1899.
   No. 7, " The Negro Artisan," 192 pp.
   1902.

8. Bulletins of the United States Depart-
ment of Labor.
Nos. 10, 14, 22, 32, 35, 37, 38, 48.

9. United States : Report of the Industrial Commission 1901–2, 19 vols.

10. Proceedings of the American Economic Association, 1906.

NOTES TO CHAPTER IV

## NOTE 18

See Atlanta University Publications, No 8, Section 4.

## NOTE 19

" Baptism doth not alter the condition of the person as to his bondage or freedom, in order that diverse masters freed from this doubt may more carefully endeavor the propagation of Christianity." (Williams I, 139.)

## NOTE 20

Cf. Dr. Albert Bushnell Hart, "The Realities of Negro Suffrage," Proceedings of the American Political Science Association, Vol. II, 1905.

## NOTE 21

The Church of England through the " Society for the Propagation of the Gospel " (incorporated 1701) sent several missionaries who worked chiefly in the North.

The history of the society goes on to say :
"It is a matter of commendation to the
clergy that they have done thus much in
so great and difficult a work. But, alas !
what is the instruction of a few hundreds in
several years with respect to the many
thousands uninstructed, unconverted, living,
dying, utter pagans. It must be confessed
what hath been done is as nothing with regard to what a true Christian would hope
to see effected." After stating several difficulties in respect to the religious instruction
of the Negroes, it is said : "But the greatest obstruction is the masters themselves do
not consider enough the obligation which
lies upon them to have their slaves instructed." The work of this society in
America ceased in 1783. The Methodists
report the following members :

| | | | | |
|---|---|---|---|---|
| 1786 | - | - | - | - | 1,890 |
| 1790 | - | - | - | - | 11,682 |
| 1791 | - | - | - | - | 12,884 |
| 1796 | - | - | - | - | 12,215 |

Nearly all were in the North and the border states. Georgia had only 148. The Baptists had 18,000 Negro members in 1793. As to the Episcopalians, the single state of Virginia where more was done than elsewhere will illustrate the result :

" The Church Commission for Work among the Colored People at a late meeting decided to request the various rectors of parishes throughout the South to institute Sunday-schools and special services for the colored population ' such as were frequently found in the South before the war.' The commission hope for ' real advance ' among the colored people in so doing. We do not agree with the commission with respect to either the wisdom or the efficiency of the plan suggested. In the first place, this ' before the war ' plan was a complete failure so far as church extension was concerned, in the past when white churchmen had complete bodily control of their slaves. . . .

" The Journals of Virginia will verify the

contention, that during the 'before the war' period, while the bishops and a large number of the clergy were always interested in the religious training of the slaves, yet as a matter of fact there was general apathy and indifference upon the part of the laity with respect to this matter.

"At various intervals resolutions were presented in the Annual Conventions with the avowed purpose of stimulating an interest in the religious welfare of the slaves. But despite all these efforts the Journals fail to record any great achievements along that line. . . . So faithful had been the work under such conditions that as late as 1879 there were less than 200 colored communicants reported in the whole state of Virginia." (*Church Advocate.*)

## NOTE 22

Charles C. Jones: "The Religious Instruction of the Negroes in the United

States," Savannah, 1842.   Cf. Atlanta University Publication, No. 8, passim.

### Note 23

Cf. Hart, *supra*.   Note too the decrease in the proportion of free Negroes.

### Note 24

Note Dr. Cartwright's articles ; DeBow's " Review," Vol. II, pp. 29, 184, 331 and 504. Cf. Fitzhugh, " Cannibals All."

### Note 25

Cf. Weeks, " Southern Quakers and Slavery," Balt. 1896 ; Ballagh, " Slavery in Virginia."

### Note 26

There has been in the North a generously conceived campaign in the last ten years to emphasize the good in the South and minimize the evil.   Consequently many people have come to believe that men like Fleming and Murphy represent either the dominant

Southern sentiment or that of a strong minority. On the contrary the brave utterances of such men represent a very small and very weak minority—a minority which is growing very slowly and which can only hope for success by means of moral support from the outside. Such moral support has not been generally given; it is Tillman, Vardaman and Dixon who get the largest hearing in the land and they represent the dominant public opinion in the South. The mass of public opinion there while it hesitates at the extreme brutality of these spokesmen is nearer to them than to Bassett or Fleming or Alderman.

## NOTE 27

Cf. " The Negro Church," Atlanta University Publication, No. 8. 212 pp. 1903.

## NOTE 28

Twenty good references on the ethical and religious aspect of slavery and the Negro problem are :

C. C. Jones, " The Religious Instruction of the Negroes in the United States," Savannah, 1842. 277 pp. 12mo.

R. F. Campbell, " Some Aspects of the Race Problem in the South," Pamphlet, 1899. Asheville, N. C. 31 pp. 8vo.

R. L. Dabney, " Defence of Virginia, and Through Her of the South," New York, 1867. 356 pp. 12mo.

Nehemiah Adams, " A South Side View of Slavery," Boston, 1854. viii, 7–214 pp. 16mo.

Richard Allen, First Bishop of the A. M. E. Church. "The life, experience and gospel labors of the Rt. Rev. Richard Allen." Written by himself. Phila., 1793. 69 pp. 8vo.

Matthew Anderson, " Presbyterianism and Its Relation to the Negro," Phila., 1897.

Geo. S. Merriam, " The Negro and the Nation," N. Y., 1906. 436 pp. 12mo.

M. S. Locke, " Anti-Slavery in America,"
255 pp.   1901.

W. A. Sinclair, " The Aftermath of Slavery," etc., with an introduction by T. W.
Higginson, Boston, 1905.   358 pp.

N. S. Shaler, " The Neighbor : The Natural   History   of   Human Contrasts " (The
problem   of   the   African),   Boston, 1904.
vii, 342 pp.   12mo.

Atlanta University Publications :

> Number   6, " The   Negro   Common
> School," 120 pp.   1901.

> Number 8, " The Negro Church," 212
> pp. 1903.

> Number 9, " Notes on Negro Crime,"
> 76 pp. 1904.

E. H. Abbott, " Religious life in America," A record of personal observation.
N. Y. : *The Outlook*, 1902.   xii, 730 pp. 8vo.

W. E. B. DuBois, " The Souls of Black
Folk," Chicago, 1903.

Friends, " A Brief Testimony of the Progress of the Friends Against Slavery and the Slave-Trade," 1671–1787.   Phila., 1843.

J. W. Hood, " One Hundred Years of the A. M. E. Zion Church."

S. M. Janney, " History of the Religious Society of Friends," Phila., 1859–1867.

D. A. Payne, " History of the A. M. E. Church," Nashville, 1891.

S. B. Weeks, " Anti-Slavery Sentiment in the South," Washington, D. C., 1898. "Southern Quakers and Slavery," Baltimore, 1896.

White, " The African Preacher."